THE FOURTH FLOOR

An Account of

the Castro Communist Revolution

The
FOURTH FLOOR

An Account of
the Castro Communist Revolution

EARL E. T. SMITH

FORMER UNITED STATES AMBASSADOR TO CUBA

Random House   New York

Third Printing

To my wife, Florence

I have donated this work to the Earl E. T. Smith Foundation which will apply the royalties to the relief of Cuban exiles in the United States.

E. E. T. S.

Contents

(*vii*)

Contents

Preface

I have undertaken to write this book because I am convinced that my experience as the United States Ambassador to Cuba was unusual in the sense that I lived through the Castro Communist Revolution, and I feel that I owe it to the American people to try to establish the fact that the Castro Communist Revolution need never have occurred. From this experience, I learned not only that our techniques of relations with Cuba were faulty but that the modus operandi for the determination of policy is not only inadequate but dangerous to the defense of our country. In Chapter 22 of this book, I summarize the conclusions reached from this experience.

When I started to work on this account of my experience as the American Ambassador to Cuba, I was troubled about my responsibilities. I had been on a governmental team; I had been appointed by President Eisenhower, I had served under Secretary of State John Foster Dulles, for both of whom I have great respect.

The men I would have to criticize were colleagues, and some of them I admire as officials and like as men. It is difficult to become so objective as to forget all these human factors. It is even more difficult to bring into the complex life of a new Administration a criticism of a great department of government which, in my judgment, requires much improvement in its housekeeping methods.

Shall I take the attitude that I was given an opportunity to have an interesting experience and keep silent? Many adopt that attitude which is the easy way. It is not in my nature to hurt others or to project my own ideas as superior to others. Why not tend to my own business, live the kind of quiet life to which I am accustomed, and leave to journalists the task of exposure?

On the other hand, I can never forget that the United States has been kind to me and to my forebears and that my first obligation is to my country. It is the way I was brought up to believe. Were it otherwise, I should never have accepted public office and I should never have taken an oath to protect and defend this country.

Therefore, I have written this book only as a footnote to history and to the science of government. It can have no other purpose.

EARL E. T. SMITH

New York, June, 1962

THE FOURTH FLOOR

An Account of

the Castro Communist Revolution

Chapter I

I Become an Ambassador

I TOOK THE OATH as United States Ambassador to Cuba on June 13, 1957, at ceremonies attended by my wife; my two daughters, Mrs. Augustus Paine II and Mrs. William Hutton; the wife of a young Senator from Massachusetts, Mrs. John F. Kennedy; the Secretary of State, John Foster Dulles; Wiley Buchanan, Chief of Protocol; and other officials of the State Department.

When not serving my government I have been actively engaged as an investment broker and corporation director. I

(3)

have retained a membership on the New York Stock Exchange for more than thirty years.

I have been active in politics both on the national level and in my home state of Florida. I have served the United States under Presidential appointment of Franklin D. Roosevelt as a dollar-a-year man on the War Production Board, and after Pearl Harbor as a member of the Armed Forces overseas during World War II. I was appointed by President Eisenhower to accompany Vice-President Nixon in January, 1956, as a member of the American delegation to the inauguration of Brazilian President Juscelino Kubitschek in Rio de Janeiro. I was appointed as President Eisenhower's Ambassador to Cuba during extremely difficult times. I was personally selected by President Kennedy to serve as Ambassador to Switzerland. Although I was honored that President Kennedy believed I could be of service to my country, I requested the President to withdraw my name because of the controversy that was stimulated.

The Swiss government represented the interests of the United States in Cuba. My opposition to Castro and his government was well known and dates back to my service in Havana. There were indications that the Swiss felt my presence in Switzerland would complicate the responsibilities their government had assumed in behalf of the United States in Cuba. Because of that, I wrote the President: "It is my judgment that our country's well being in this matter would best be served if my name were removed from consideration as Ambassador to Switzerland."

Cuba was a diplomatic assignment I had long wanted. My interest in Cuba was never a superficial one; since 1928 I had been visiting there. The people and the country were familiar to me and I had many Cuban friends. I have spoken French and German since childhood. I studied Spanish at the Foreign Service School and continued my Spanish lessons at the Embassy in Havana. I had traveled widely and knew Cuba well, and I felt I could judge the thoughts and moods of the Cuban people because of the close relationship I had enjoyed in the islands for so many years. I was fully aware the assignment would be a challenge, but this only stimulated my interest further.

I knew, even before I went to Cuba, that I would have to deal with the Castro revolution. I did not know then that this was a Communist revolution and I was informed neither by the officials of the State Department nor by Herbert Matthews of the *New York Times,* from whom I was instructed to receive a briefing, that the observation of the Castro Communist revolution would be my responsibility.

I now know that those in charge of Cuban affairs in the State Department were advised from many other sources of the Communist infiltration of the 26th of July Movement [1] and of the Communist sympathizers who held important positions in the Movement, especially among the troops led by Raúl Castro.

From the time Castro landed in the Province of Oriente in December 1956, the State Department received reports of probable Communist infiltration and exploitation of the 26th of July Movement. The State Department was aware of Castro's contacts with Communists in Mexico. Certain officials in the State Department were familiar with Castro's part in the bloody Communist-inspired uprising in Bogotá, known as the "Bogotazo" of 1948. In addition to my reports and information from many outside sources, the State Department also had reports from its own Bureau of Research and Intelligence.

This knowledge was not made available to the American

[1] The name originates from the attack on the Moncada barracks in Santiago on July 26, 1953, which was led by Fidel Castro and Raúl Castro.

people. I am now convinced that neither President Eisenhower nor Secretary of State John Foster Dulles were provided with information available to officials in the State Department and the Central Intelligence Agency (CIA).

My official briefings included a lengthy conversation in New York City with Herbert Matthews. This briefing was suggested to me by William Wieland, Director of the Office of Caribbean and Mexican Affairs, and approved by Roy R. Rubottom, Assistant Secretary of State for Latin American Affairs.

Mr. Matthews informed me that he had very knowledgeable views of Cuba and Latin America in general. He was of the firm belief that it would be in the best interests of Cuba and the rest of the world if Batista were removed from office. Mr. Matthews had a very poor opinion of Batista. He considered him a Rightist, ruthless, and corrupt dictator.

The significance of my briefing by Mr. Matthews is that it revealed the thinking and the aims of those influential sources in the lower echelon of the State Department at that time, for the views of the *New York Times* journalist on the Cuba situation were fully publicized. In February 1957, Herbert Matthews visited Fidel Castro in the hills of the Sierra Maestra. As a result, he wrote three articles on Fidel Castro which appeared as lead columns on the front page of the *New York Times* on three separate days. The newspaper also carried photographs of Fidel Castro and Herbert Matthews to dispel the rumors of Castro's death. In these articles, Matthews eulogized Fidel Castro, portrayed him as a political Robin Hood, and compared him to Abraham Lincoln.

On August 30, 1960, in reply to questioning before a subcommittee of the Judiciary Committee of the United States Senate, as to what part, if any, the United States played in Castro's and the Communist rise to power in Cuba, I testified:

(6)

I Become an Ambassador

The United States Government agencies and the United States press played a major role in bringing Castro to power.

Three front page articles in the *New York Times* in early 1957 written by the editorialist, Herbert Matthews, served to inflate Castro to world stature and world recognition. Until that time, Castro had been just another bandit in the Oriente Mountains of Cuba with a handful of followers who had terrorized the campesinos, that is, the peasants throughout the countryside.

Fidel Castro landed on the south coast of Oriente in December of 1956, from Mexico, with an expeditionary force of eighty-one men. Intercepted by Cuban gunboats and patrol planes, Castro and a handful of stragglers managed to ensconce themselves in the rugged eight-thousand-foot Sierra Maestra Range.

After the Matthews articles which followed an exclusive interview by the *Times* editorial writer in Castro's mountain hideout and which likened him to Abraham Lincoln, he was able to get followers and funds in Cuba and in the United States. From that time on, arms, money and soldiers of fortune abounded. Much of the American press began to picture Castro as a political Robin Hood.

Before leaving Washington I made an appointment with the Secretary of State, John Foster Dulles, to pay my respects to this distinguished gentleman. As he was preparing for a visit to Europe, our meeting was brief. Yet he had time to convince me of his appreciation of Cuba's friendship for the United States, so clearly and so often demonstrated by Cuba's Ambassador to the United Nations, Dr. Emilio Núñez Portuondo. As I left the Secretary's office, I could not help but reflect over his words. I was impressed by the difference of the Secretary's attitude toward the government of Cuba as compared to the impressions I had acquired during my extended period of briefing in the lower echelon, often referred to as the Fourth Floor.

My final instructions from the State Department were to

travel around the country, see the people, and let the Cubans know that I wanted to get generally acquainted with them and their customs.

I arrived in Havana on the S.S. *Grand Haven* on July 15, 1957, from Palm Beach, Florida, accompanied by my wife, our son, his nurse and our dog.

Chapter II

The Early Days

BETWEEN AMBASSADOR ARTHUR GARDNER'S DEPARTURE from and my arrival in Havana there was a matter of three or four weeks. On our arrival, I found an atmosphere of excitement. I also was moved by the feeling of hope on the part of the people that the appointment of a new Ambassador indicated a new attitude toward the government of Cuba on the part of the United States.

Some of the people of Cuba thought my appointment might presage direct intervention in the tumultuous political affairs of their country. However, my departure from the

United States had been purposely delayed to avoid the inference this appointment was of an emergency character.

Immediately on our arrival in Cuba, we were informed three bombs had been found on the grounds of the Hotel National, where we were to spend our first six weeks while the Embassy residence was being prepared. It was the belief of Minister Counselor Vinton Chapin, who was soon to leave Cuba to assume his new post as United States Ambassador to Luxembourg, and other officers of the Embassy, that the bombs had been placed by the 26th of July Movement to remind our government there was an active opposition against the government of Cuba. However, the revolutionaries sent messages to the Embassy, by courier, maintaining the bombs had been placed by government officials to impress upon the Ambassador the terroristic nature of Castro's revolutionary movement. I was thus immediately involved in the fiery surge of Cuban politics.

At my first staff meeting of the principal aides of the Embassy, I told them frankly that I realized mine was to be a post at which no Ambassador could win, for, to be correct, the American Ambassador should be strictly impartial in the internal affairs of the country to which he is assigned. On the one side, the American government had been criticized for attempting to perpetuate the Batista dictatorship. On the other hand, I was the accredited American representative to the friendly government of Cuba under Fulgéncio Batista.

I knew Cubans well enough to realize you must be either with them or against them. To be strictly impartial meant neither side would like you. I was prepared to accept the situation, and I said my actions would be guided only by what I deemed was in the best interest of the United States.

One of my first acts was to issue instructions that no cables were to leave the Embassy without my approval. This procedure was always followed. If I were unavailable, cables had then to be submitted to the Deputy Chief of Mission, Vinton Chapin, and, later, to Minister Counselor Daniel E. Braddock. I regretted the departure of Minister Counselor Chapin to assume his post as Ambassador to Luxembourg. He was replaced as Deputy Chief of Mission by Minister Counselor Braddock, an able, loyal and conscientious officer of the State Department.

At eleven o'clock on the morning of July 24th, I held my first press conference at the American Embassy in Havana. The conference lasted one hour and fifteen minutes and all the large Cuban dailies were represented (there were nineteen in Havana alone), as were international wire services, news magazines, and newsreels. The Conference Room on the top floor of the Embassy was jammed. Seated beside me at a long table were First Secretary John Topping, Minister Counselor Chapin, and an Embassy Spanish-speaking interpreter. The technique I selected to meet the press was first to make a general statement and then open the conference to questions.

My opening statement was:

I want you to know that Mrs. Smith and I are extremely pleased to be in Cuba. We both are busily studying Spanish. I am proud to have been chosen for this assignment by President Eisenhower. We admire this country and the Cuban people, and intend to get to other parts of the island often, to know both better. As a matter of fact, I plan to visit Santiago de Cuba, Moa Bay, Nicaro, and our naval base at Guantánamo Bay, with some members of my staff the middle of next week.

I am dedicated to the task of maintaining and strengthening the fine relations between our two countries. Cubans and Americans have fought side by side on several occasions in defense of democratic ideals, and the two nations, I feel, will always be the closest of friends, and allies in the common fight against Communist subversion. Cuba is as loyal and has been as good a friend of the United

States as any of our sister nations. I shall certainly work toward strengthening that fine relationship.

After the statement, the conference was opened to questions. I went on to say that

The basic policy of the United States toward Cuba is non-intervention in the internal affairs of Cuba. We are as close as any other two peoples in the world, not only geographically, but in kinship. I am confident that the Cuban people are peace-loving and I hope they can solve their problems in their own way, for Cuban problems are for the Cuban people to solve, without outside intervention.[1]

Naturally, there was immediate, close questioning from the press, regarding which Cuban political factions I would receive at the Embassy, and socially at the Embassy residence. I reiterated, "I am prepared to receive and talk with anyone who approaches me through normal channels, with the objective of explaining his views, but I will hold no clandestine meetings."

Another member of the press pursued the same subject, couched in different language, for, with the stirring, churning political situation in Cuba, it was of utmost interest who would be received by the United States Ambassador. They wanted to know precisely which opposition leaders would be invited to confer with me at the Embassy. I was asked, "Do you mean you will receive and talk to any and all leaders of any and all opposition parties, including those dedicated to the overthrow of the present government of Cuba by force?" [2]

I repeated emphatically, "I will hold no clandestine meetings, but I will talk with anyone who approaches me through normal channels with the objective of explaining his views."

During this conference, I tried to answer all questions

[1] *Times* of Havana, July 25, 1957.
[2] *Times* of Havana, July 25, 1957.

with frankness. On only this one issue of which opposition leaders would be received in conference at the Embassy was I forced to beg off on the grounds that I had stated my case and further discussion might lead to misunderstanding. For a newly appointed Ambassador to have been specific would indeed have been undiplomatic and could serve no purpose in future relations with the government to which I had been accredited or to the opposition parties.

The conference moved on to other issues. Questioned on whether I thought Batista was fighting communism in Cuba in a manner satisfactory to the United States State Department, I replied: "The United States is gratified by the decisive moves made by the government of Cuba to outlaw the Communist Party, sever diplomatic relations with Russia and establish a Bureau for the Repression of Communist Activities (BRAC). I am confident the Cuban people are too intelligent to pay attention to, or be taken in by, Communist lies and false promises."

I elaborated, "The United States and the American people appreciate, with admiration and respect, the position taken by Cuba's delegate to the United Nations, Dr. Núñez Portuondo, in the historic speech he delivered in criticism of Russia's role in the suppression of the Hungarian revolt last Fall (1956). We take his words as an indication of the feelings of the Cuban people toward Communism."

The press now switched to personal and humorous questions. An outstanding trait of Cuban personality is a sense of humor, active at even the most intense moments. The American Ambassador in Cuba held a position second only to the President of Cuba because of our vast business, cultural and social ties. Therefore, the Cuban people were singularly curious about background, family, hobbies, family pets—all points almost embarrassingly reminiscent of the American interest in motion picture stars.

The conference dispersed on a light vein. I was amused to be asked by Ted Scott, columnist for the *Havana Post*, and who, in months to come, proved to be a reliable and valuable friend, "Ambassador, as a former champion boxer in college, do you favor the overthrow of the present world heavyweight boxing champion by Cuban challenger, Nino Valdes, by force?"

Before an Ambassador presents his credentials to the Chief of State of a nation to which he is to be accredited, it is customary for the Embassy to submit the Ambassador's speech of introduction to the Foreign Office of that country. This is done so the Chief of State may have sufficient time to prepare a suitable response.

My original speech of introduction, prepared by the Embassy and the Department of State, stated that the people of the United States were deeply saddened by the blood now being shed in Cuba, and it was the fervent hope of all Americans that Cuba would find a peaceful solution to its problems. When the speech was delivered to the Foreign Office, it caused concern, for such an introductory remark indicated the United States Government did not believe the government of Cuba could control the political situation in the island. Such a statement was undiplomatic. Fortunately, I received instructions to recall the document and delete the disparaging words. As far as the public was concerned, no harm was done, for there was no leakage. But Batista, who already had a copy of the speech, knew the State Department had indicated through these words their stiffening attitude toward his government.

On the morning of July 23, I presented my credentials to President Batista as Ambassador Extraordinary and Plenipotentiary of the United States to Cuba. The short, dignified ceremony, based on century-old procedures, took place in the Hall of Mirrors in the Presidential Palace at eleven thirty in the morning. Ladies were not allowed to attend.

In Cuba my wife was the first Ambassador's wife ever to observe the entire ceremony. The President broke this long-established precedent by inviting her to observe the ceremony from a small balcony overlooking a vast room with a magnificent vaulted ceiling.

Little did I realize at the time that eighteen months later I would be visiting in the same room with Fidel Castro's designee for President of the Provisional Government, Manuel Urrutia!

Accompanied by a delegation of seven military and civilian officials of the United States Embassy, I presented my credentials to President Batista. In my speech of introduction, I told the President that it was my intention to make a tour of Cuba, "as soon as I had the chance—to get to know the country and the people." I stated that I had been "an admirer of Cuba for a long time," emphasizing that I felt "true affection for the Cuban people."

President Batista replied that he learned with pleasure that on some future occasion I intended to travel through the island in order to know more about the country and the Cubans. The Cuban President said that my intentions to tour Cuba reminded him of similar visits he made while living in the United States. He said: "I have the most pleasant impressions of your country." And added: "I do not forget, and I cherish the remembrance that, notwithstanding the fact that I was then a political exile, I was able to obtain, through my conduct, the respect of my neighbors there, for Cuba and for myself, doubtless because I never attempted to break the pattern of life, or the laws of the country, the generous hospitality of which I was enjoying."

Following the speech, President Batista and I enjoyed a brief chat, at which time President Batista again emphasized his pleasure at my intention of touring Cuba. This was my first meeting with President Batista. He impressed me as being a tough guy with bull-like strength and exuding a forceful, agreeable personality. Here was an extraordinary example of a virile man of the soil and of mixed antecedents, who had projected himself from a simple sergeant to the Presidency of his country.

As we left the Palace, the battalion of artillery troops snapped to attention and presented arms while the band played "The Star-Spangled Banner." President Batista stood on the balcony of the Palace and waved good-by as our cars drove off.

Chapter III

The Santiago Incident

IT IS THE CUSTOM for the Ambassador who has just arrived at a new post to give a reception for the members of the Embassy staff. The Embassy residence unfortunately was not ready for occupancy, so my wife and I held our reception at the Hotel National on July 17, two days after our arrival.

At this party, in a conversation between First Secretary for Political Affairs John Topping, Minister Counselor Vinton Chapin and myself, it was decided that we should leave before the end of the month on a trip to include Santiago in Oriente Province; our Guantánamo Naval Base; the American-owned Moa Bay Mining Company properties (subsidiary of Freeport Sulphur), with an investment of approximately seventy-five million dollars; and the United States Government Nickel properties at Nicaro with an investment of over one hundred million dollars.

Once the trip was announced on July 25, six days before our departure, the mold was cast. It was announced sufficiently early to permit the government to prepare the climate for the visit. It also gave the opposition time to prepare for a demonstration. The trip was arranged to conform with my instructions to get around the island. It was approved by the State Department and by President Batista.

At approximately eight o'clock the night before our scheduled departure, I was informed that a 26th of July leader and a prominent businessman, Frank Pais and Raúl Pujol, had been shot and killed in Santiago by government forces. When I received the news, I was attending a staff members' reception in honor of a departing Foreign Service officer. We wondered if the event was accidental, or might the shooting have been done for the purpose of getting me to call off the trip to Oriente. The possibility of postponing the trip was considered.

If it was postponed, the revolutionaries would claim the government shot the men to prevent the trip. After consultation with members of the Embassy staff, the decision was made to go through with the trip.

We left Havana on the Embassy Air Attaché plane on the morning of July 31 at 7:00 A.M., arriving at Santiago at 10:30. The members of the party included Mrs. Smith, three military service attachés, the Second Secretary for Economic Affairs, the First Secretary for Political Affairs, the outgoing and incoming public affairs officers, and the Chief Intelligence Officer. We proceeded to Santiago's colonial City Hall, where I was presented with the keys of the city.

Our arrival in Santiago, which is the capital of Oriente

Province and the second largest city in Cuba, was made while the population was emotionally disturbed, supposedly because of the shooting. A general strike of Santiago businessmen had closed down the city. That afternoon, the funeral of the two prominent revolutionaries was to take place. Thousands took part in the funeral procession.

As my wife and I entered the City Hall, a man pushed forward and thrust three rolls of film in her hand. He begged her to carry them out of Santiago. She had to refuse.

While I was receiving the keys to the city of Santiago de Cuba, and the customary speeches were taking place, you could hear a growing roar of voices outside. The mothers of Santiago were demonstrating in the square. A group of approximately two hundred women—some quite young and, to all appearances, representative of the upper middle class—staged a demonstration in Parque Céspedes in front of the Municipal Palace. The women were dressed completely in black. Many were too young to have been mothers of grown sons. They were obviously recruited for the occasion. The demonstrators were singing the Cuban national anthem, and shouting, "Liberty! Liberty!" The women, in attempting to break through the police lines, brought down the wrath of the police and the Army Intelligence men upon them. Fire engines arrived and the firemen turned the hoses on the women. The police unnecessarily beat them back with their clubs.

Our audience became bored with the speeches and moved to the large windows overlooking the square in front of the Municipal Palace. As soon as Mrs. Smith and I came out of the City Hall onto the street, the demonstration increased. Some of the women were successful in breaking through the lines and getting to us. The mothers of Santiago became hysterical and fought to get to me. We were appalled by the unnecessary roughness and brutality of the police. Some women were knocked down, others were thrown in the police wagon.

Newsmen asked my reaction to the events. I said, "I think it unfortunate that some of the people of Santiago de Cuba took advantage of my presence here to demonstrate and protest to their own government." The press was not satisfied. Did I approve of such brutality and was the attitude of the American Embassy toward the Batista government to be the same as under Ambassador Gardner? The press intimated that my statement could be interpreted as inferring approval of the method by which the demonstration was quelled.

Here was an occasion at Santiago when an envoy must make an on-the-spot decision. I told the newsmen there would be a press conference after lunch.

It was our belief that if the Santiago incident had not occurred a situation similar to that in Santiago would have had to be faced sooner or later. It was common knowledge throughout the island that my predecessor, Ambassador Arthur Gardner, and Mrs. Gardner, had been close personal friends of President Batista, even to playing canasta several times a week. The opposition maintained that Ambassador Gardner had been too friendly to Batista.

I realized that a delicate diplomatic point had been raised and had to be met. The question had been brought to a head and could not be avoided. My instructions from the State Department had been to alter the prevailing notion in Cuba that the American Ambassador was intervening on behalf of the government of Cuba to perpetuate the Batista dictatorship. The government seemed to have acquired a feeling that a "new deal" was being initiated by the State Department. The government of Cuba wanted to know where it stood. Therefore, both the opposition and the government were anxious for a showdown on the new Ambassador's attitude. Both sides were trying to use for their advantage anything I said or did. Both sides got the answer at Santiago—that I was not for one side or the other, but that I was impartial in the Cuban political struggle.

After a luncheon at Santiago's Rancho Club Restaurant in the hilly outskirts of the city, at an informal press conference, I issued the following statement:

I would like to make the preliminary observation that I feel that some of the people of Santiago de Cuba took advantage of my presence here to demonstrate and protest to their own government.

As I said in my press conference on July 25, the American people are saddened and concerned over the political unrest which has led to bloodshed in Cuba. I have received a letter signed by the Mothers of Santiago de Cuba. This will receive my careful attention and consideration.

Any form of excessive police action is abhorrent to me. I deeply regret that my presence in Santiago de Cuba may have been the cause of public demonstrations which brought on police retaliation. I sincerely trust that those held by the police as a result of their demonstrations have been released.

In response to a question as to the purpose of my visit, I said that: "It was not purely for courtesy but to inform myself and that I had latitude from my Government in that regard."

In response to a further question, I added that: "I had latitude to observe and report, not, repeat, not to intervene." With these words, the press conference ended.

While the funeral of the revolutionaries at Santiago was taking place in the afternoon, I visited the cemetery to lay a wreath on the tomb of Cuba's national hero, José Martí.

In the city of Santiago, the funeral of Pais and Pujol turned into a spontaneous general strike. From their hideouts in the hills, Castro's guerrillas pounced upon isolated military outposts at Minas and Bueycito. They ambushed the soldiers, captured their arms and ammunition and set fire to the large sugar mill at Maceo.

That evening we dined quietly at the home of the United States Consul, Oscar Guerra, and were informed that a dispatch had been given out reporting the release of more than thirty women who had been arrested in the morning during the demonstration at Parque Céspedes.

Early the next morning, August 1, we left for the United States Naval Base at Guantánamo Bay. Following the full honors accredited to the rank of Ambassador, the Admiral introduced me to the heads of departments and other senior officers of the Base who were present and in formation. I then went on a complete tour of this huge United States Naval Base, one of the principal American Naval Bases outside the continental limits of the United States. We spent that night at the Base and had a delightful time with Admiral Ellis, Mrs. Ellis, and the staff officers.

Once again, civilian laws in Cuba were suspended. President Fulgéncio Batista, on the first of August, suspended constitutional guarantees throughout Cuba for a period of forty-five days. Under the suspension of constitutional guarantees, the government assumed the authority to search homes without warrant, arrest citizens and hold them without trial. Under the same power, the government imposed censorship of the press and radio.

I was suddenly confronted with the possibility of discontinuing the trip. The statement at the Santiago press conference had created a furor. The words "Any form of excessive police action is abhorrent to me" became explosive. Batista objected to this, and some of his friends began a campaign to have me recalled. The government newspapers attacked me viciously. The press in the United States reprinted the attacks published in the Cuban government press. I decided to ignore the tempest, to carry on the trip as planned, and to make my full report to the State Department after the trip was completed and I had returned to Havana.

The following day, August 2, we left for the Moa Bay Mining Company and the Nicaro Nickel properties. In these high hills, covered with pine trees, lie vast reserves of iron ore. The United States government and the Freeport Sulphur Company invested separately a total of $175,000,000 for the production of nickel in these properties.

My trip to Santiago demonstrated that everything the United States and its Ambassadors did, or did not do, in Latin America, affects the internal political situations of these countries. It needs to be pointed out and stressed that every act on the part of an American diplomat and every word spoken officially, and sometimes unofficially, in a country like Cuba, was considered political intervention, and such words were magnified far beyond their importance. All this made the task of an Ambassador particularly difficult. Before Castro, the United States was so important in the minds of the Cuban people that the American Ambassador was, to repeat, regarded as the second most important personage in Cuba. He was a symbol of both power and friendship.

The close relationship between our two countries goes back many years. The United States and Cuba fought side by side in the Spanish-American War of 1898. At his country home, Finca Kuquine, President Batista proudly displayed to me the original letter, written in 1902, from President Theodore Roosevelt to President Estrada Palma of Cuba. It was a letter of congratulation because Cuba had gained its independence.

Our relations with Cuba for many years were based upon the Platt Amendments which were added to the Army Appropriation Bill of March 2, 1901. On May 22, 1903, the Cuban Convention duly added them as an appendix to the Cuban

Constitution. To protect elimination by the amending power, the Platt Amendments were also incorporated into a treaty between the United States and Cuba on May 22, 1903. These amendments, which gave the United States the right to intervene in Cuba's internal affairs, were in effect until May 29, 1934, when they were ended by a mutual statement of abrogation. After that, Cuba achieved full sovereignty. While our legal status in Cuba was thus weakened, our prestige and significance were strengthened.

After my return to Havana, I was gratified to learn that the Secretary of State, John Foster Dulles, at a press conference in Washington, warmly defended me and my statement made at Santiago. He said:

> I read the statement and I want to say that it is a statement which, perhaps from a purely technical point of view, may not have been perfectly correct. But it was a human statement. I am glad we have some, in fact, I hope many Ambassadors who are not mere automatic machines but who do have sentiments of humanity which they sometimes express without regard, perhaps, to the diplomatic niceties. His statement was a very well balanced statement and he made it because he felt that he had become involved in, and had been a cause of, the trouble. He regretted, on the one hand, that his visit had been used to stage demonstrations, and he regretted, on the other hand, that the restraining of those demonstrators had involved certain, what he regarded as, police brutalities. And a person of flesh and blood and heart would, I think, under the circumstances of the case, have made the kind of statement that he did. I am confident that even if it was, in certain technical respects, perhaps not correct, that there will be an understanding of it on the part of the authorities in Cuba, because it was a very human thing to do and, as I say, we want our Ambassadors to be human people.

The following editorial appeared in the *New York Times* on August 3, 1957:

The Santiago Incident

It was good to hear Secretary of State Dulles on Tuesday stand up for our new Ambassador to Cuba, Earl E. T. Smith. The Secretary's remarks were also not without their importance both as an expression of the technique of diplomacy and as an implied attitude toward the military dictatorship of President Batista.

With the introduction of telephone, teletype, cable and radio communications, diplomacy has lost much of its personal flavor. An Ambassador may have the title of "Plenipotentiary," but his powers are rarely evolved and executed on the spot.

However, there are occasions when an envoy is called upon for a snap judgment. Mr. Smith faced such an occasion in Santiago de Cuba on July 31. His visit had inspired a peaceful anti-Batista demonstration by two hundred women of the city. Mr. Smith saw the police treat the women brutally and learned that thirty of them had been arrested. He naturally felt a sense of responsibility and outrage and, as "a person of flesh and blood and heart would" (to quote Mr. Dulles), the Ambassador protested against the "excessive police action" and expressed the hope that the women arrested would be released—as they were.

This—again to cite Mr. Dulles—"may not have been perfectly correct" from the traditional diplomatic standpoint, but it was "a very human statement." It also was a courageous one. Cuban-American relations had deteriorated seriously before Mr. Smith arrived. He did more to restore happy relations in one stroke than the most skillful traditional diplomacy could have done in many months.

Does this mean that the State Department's attitude toward the dictatorial regime of President Batista has changed? Cubans evidently now believe so. The change of Ambassadors and the attitude of Mr. Smith are taken as indications. So will be Mr. Dulles' support of Ambassador Smith and his refusal to express an opinion about the political situation in Cuba when he was asked to do so on Wednesday.

A curtain of darkness descended on Cuba with the imposition of complete censorship on August 1. It is significant that the last piece of news to come out of Cuba free of censorship concerned Ambassador Smith's stand for decency and democracy. There may well have been a connection between what happened in Santiago

de Cuba and the suspension the next day of constitutional guarantees. The door was closed too late.

These were the last complimentary words I was to receive
from the *New York Times* and their Latin American expert,
Herbert Matthews. The clearer I saw Fidel Castro in his true
colors, the more I alienated Herbert Matthews.

On September 1, 1957, I attended the horse races at
Oriental Park, Havana, because they had named a handicap
in my honor. Hundreds of Cuban people stood up and cheered
as I entered. According to Cuban newspapers it was one of
the greatest ovations ever given an individual in the forty-two-
year history of the race track.

The ovation was not a personal tribute, nor was it recognition of any virtues as an individual, but an eager tribute to
an American respect of humanity, so clearly expressed at Santiago.

Chapter IV

Difficulties with Batista

BECAUSE OF THE FUROR of the Santiago Incident a diplomatically uncomfortable relationship existed for several weeks, and I realized that it was up to me to restore normal diplomatic relations with Batista. At a reception given at the Haitian Embassy, I saw Foreign Minister Gonzalo Guell and asked for an interview with the President of the Republic.

The interview was arranged by the Foreign Minister, and I met the President of the Republic at the Palace two days later. We talked frankly and freely for more than two hours. During my entire mission, this was the only official call I made

on Batista in the Presidential Palace. All other official conferences were held in the late evenings at his country home,
Finca Kuquine, just outside of Havana.

At this meeting, I explained to Batista the circumstances
and reasons for my Santiago statement, to which his government had taken exception. At first he protested that I was the
accredited American Ambassador to his government; therefore, my "constancy" while in Cuba was to him. I told him
diplomatically, that the Embassy had been accused of being
too close to him. We were accused by the opposition of per-
petuating his regime and that my instructions were to restore
the American Embassy in the minds of Cubans to an impartial basis in the difficult political times through which Cuba
was passing. I pointed out to the President the pressure which
was being exerted on the Department of State because of the
Embassy's over-friendly relationship with him. When I asked
Batista if his actions, or reactions, would have been any different in my circumstances at Santiago, he finally said he agreed
with and understood my position.

I had accomplished my first mission of establishing the
Embassy's position of impartiality in the political affairs of
Cuba. Our exchange of views also re-established satisfactory
diplomatic relations between our two countries.

I began to expand my contacts and to concentrate on my
second mission—to persuade Batista to restore constitutional
guarantees and to lift the press censorship.

Chapter V

Fidel Castro and the CIA

I MADE AN INTENSIVE STUDY into the background of Fidel Castro. I spent days talking to people who had known him from childhood. It was the unanimous opinion of these people that Fidel was an unstable terrorist. I was careful during this searching and exhaustive study to listen to sound and intelligent Cubans who were anti-Batista. They were outstanding professional men, intellectual leaders, and the clergy. No matter how anti-Batista these people were, they believed Castro would be worse for Cuba than Batista.

It is incorrect to assume that the only opposition to Batista was Castro and his followers. A powerful anti-Batista element existed that was not terroristic. It represented the middle class and the intelligentsia of the country. I regarded this as the legal opposition, and included in this element were men who were capable of governing the country. We threw the Embassy open to all trends of political thought, including the legal opposition. However, our doors were not open to the revolutionaries who were attempting to overthrow the government by force.

In my testimony before the Senate Sub-Committee on Internal Security on August 30, 1960, the following colloquy took place:

Senator Eastland: You had been warning the State Department that Castro was a Marxist?

Mr. Smith: Yes, sir.

Senator Eastland: And that Batista's government was a friendly government. That is what had been your advice to the State Department?

Mr. Smith: Let me answer that this way—which will make it very clear. When I went to Cuba, I left here with the definite feeling according to my briefings which I had received, that the United States Government was too close to the Batista regime, and that we were being accused of intervening in the affairs of Cuba by trying to perpetuate the Batista dictatorship.

After I had been in Cuba for approximately two months, and had made a study of Fidel Castro and the revolutionaries, it was perfectly obvious to me, as it would be to any other reasonable man, that Castro was not the answer, that if Castro came to power it would not be in the best interests of Cuba or in the best interests of the United States.

Unfortunately, some of the officers in the Havana Embassy continued until the end to believe that Castro was the salvation for Cuba. There was a lapse of time of approximately one month between the time of Ambassador Gardner's departure and my arrival in Cuba. During that period, the Embassy in Havana notified the State Department that the Batista government was brushing off all the opposition as Communists, and reported that labeling the opposition as Communists was standard policy on the part of the government of Cuba.

On September 5, 1957, at the naval base in Cienfuegos in Las Villas Province, Cuban naval officers, with the mutual assistance of civilian revolutionaries, launched their biggest uprising up to that time against the Batista government. The American Embassy was informed of the over-all preparations for the insurrection. The planning was to be co-ordinated between the naval bases in Havana and Cienfuegos.

Those in authority at Havana postponed the date for launching, but failed to notify the insurrectionists at the Cienfuegos naval base. Rebellious elements were able to seize and control the base and they were successful in taking over control of the entire city for some hours in co-operation with the armed civilian revolutionaries. Bombers were dispatched to the naval base from Camp Columbia. Some of the pilots, not wishing to kill their confrères, released their bombs at sea. Troops and tanks converged on Cienfuegos to squash the resistance. Total dead were estimated in excess of three hundred.

Although the revolt was a failure and was crushed, it made Batista and his government officials realize that they no longer were able to count on the blind support of the armed forces, which Batista had previously completely depended upon.

Our information on the revolt came to us through our No. 2 CIA man in the Embassy, whose activities in giving aid and comfort to the Castro forces was disclosed at the court-martial of the naval officers who participated in the revolt. At this trial, it was divulged that an officer of the American Embassy had advised the revolutionaries that, if the revolution were successful and Batista overthrown, the United States would recognize the revolutionaries. This gave much moral encouragement to the rebels.

Although all American officials, no matter to which service they are attached, are under the authority of the Ambassador and are supposed to report to him, I knew nothing of this CIA man's activities. He acted on his own. I doubt that the Secretary of State was informed of this incident.

I quote from my testimony before the Senate Sub-Committee:

Mr. Sourwine: Mr. Smith, you spoke earlier of the No. 2 CIA man in your mission having been caught giving aid and comfort to the Castro forces. Would you tell us just what he did?

Mr. Smith: Yes. In September, 1957, the navy had an uprising at Cienfuegos, Cuba. We in the American Embassy were familiar that a revolt of some type would take place. That information came to us through the CIA, or some other source in the Embassy.

If I may divert for a minute, that is the trouble with Cubans; they talk too much. We did not know when it was going to take place.

We finally heard that the revolt at Cienfuegos had been called off. However, the navy in Havana forgot to notify the navy at Cienfuegos, and they went on with the revolt, while the navy in Havana did not participate.

This revolt was squashed by the Batista government.

In the trial of the naval officers, it came out that the No. 2 man had said that if the revolution were successful, the United States would recognize the revolutionaries.

I do not believe that the No. 2 man in the CIA intended to convey that thought. His story to me was that he had been called over to interview some men believed to be doctors, because they were dressed in white coats, and when they advised him of the revolt that was to take place, they wanted to know what the position of the United States would be.

And he inadvertently intimated, something to the effect of

which I am not quite sure, that the United States might give recognition.

As soon as the Embassy learned of this, I called a meeting of the Embassy staff and laid down the law that [neither] the Ambassador, nor anyone [else], could give [any statement] as to whom the United States would recognize; that there were only two people in the United States who had that authority:

One was the Secretary of State and the other was the President of the United States.

The information of what had taken place was brought to me by Batista. Batista was very indignant. However, I explained what [had] happened and told him—Batista—that the CIA man had done this inadvertently and had not realized what he was saying or to whom he was talking.

Batista was co-operative and did not ask to have the man leave the country.

In September 1957, I asked the Chief of the CIA Section attached to the Embassy to review their figures on Communist Party strength in Cuba—both as to card-bearing Communists and Communist sympathizers.

I questioned our estimates because nine years earlier, when the Communists for the last time in Cuba voted as a party under the Communist label, they polled over one hundred and twenty thousand votes and Juan Marinello was the candidate. Nevertheless, the Embassy CIA estimates on Communist Party strength in Cuba in 1957 indicated only ten thousand card-bearing Communists, and approximately 20,000 odd Communist sympathizers.

It is interesting to note that the CIA officer had a closed mind and demonstrated a resentment to my references to Fidel, which I made on numerous occasions at our morning staff meetings. At these meetings, I used to refer to Fidel Castro as the "outlaw" and the "bandit leader" in the hills. In jest I asked him from time to time if he was not a *"Fidelista"* (Fidel Castro supporter).

These feelings of resentment were shown by a remark he made when he walked out of my office. After I had asked him to review the figures, I heard him say, "We don't care what you think." I realized this remark may have come out inadvertently—like a hiccup. Yet it also indicated the intellectual snobbism directed by the career officers against the political appointees.

This officer was later transferred to another post. The decision was made in Washington of CIA's own volition because he had been too long at the Havana Embassy.

The career officers and the foreign service officers are the professionals of the State Department. They are proud, and have an understandable esprit de corps. There is an inevitable resentment amongst these professionals against a political appointee—be he an Ambassador, an Assistant Secretary of State, an Under Secretary of State, or even a Secretary of State. The professionals feel that the political appointees are here today and gone tomorrow.

On April 3, 1958, the Chief of the Central American Bureau of the CIA visited the Embassy in Havana after a visit in Panama and Venezuela. He told me that he shared my fear of the Communist influence in Cuba. The CIA was cognizant of the Communist ties with Raúl Castro and Che Guevara. Yet it is significant that the CIA was not concerned about Fidel Castro himself being a Communist.

Nearly eleven months after Castro came to power on November 5, 1959, the following exchange of views took place before the Internal Security Sub-Committee of the United States Senate between Senator Olin D. Johnston and General C. P. Cabell (Deputy Director of the Central Intelligence Agency):

Senator Johnston: Is it not true that he (Castro) is more dangerous than if he would come out and let them know that he was a Communist?

General Cabell: I personally would agree that Castro would probably lose much, or even most, of his popular support should this occur. However, we believe Castro is not a member of the Communist Party, and does not consider himself to be a Communist.

Senator Johnston: He knows himself that, if he would come out openly for the Communists, he would lose his usefulness.

General Cabell: That is right. In so far as he loses public support, he loses the capability to achieve his goals—though he could still be portrayed as victim of counter-revolutionary machinations.

Several months after I assumed my post as Chief of Mission in Havana, I sent a telegram to Allen Dulles, Director of the Central Intelligence Agency marked, "Allen Dulles' Eyes Only." The telegram recommended the placing of an agent in the top echelon of the Fidel Castro forces, then hiding in the Sierra Maestra hills, so that the CIA could keep themselves informed as to the extent of Communist infiltration and as to the extent of Communist control of the Castro movement (26th of July Movement). I must assume that this was never done, or they would have been better informed.

Chapter VI

The Tight Rope

AT FIRST, the members of the American colony were afraid that I was seeing too much of the opposition. They noted that I played golf with former Cuban Ambassador to the United States, Luis Machado; and Washington representative to the Cuban sugar industry, Joaquin Meyer, both of whom were known to be anti-Batista. American business interests were pro-government of Cuba, because the government of Cuba was giving them protection against the sabotage efforts of the terrorists and the raiding and looting of the revolutionaries.

Shortly after my arrival in Cuba, French Ambassador

Philippe Grousset gave an official dinner for my wife and myself. Former Prime Minister, Jorge García Montes, refused to attend. Other officials of the government of Cuba were afraid to be seen with me because they felt that my sympathies were not with Batista.

As my sympathies appeared to lean toward Castro when I first arrived in Cuba, Foreign Minister Guell confided later that he had written to the United States to make inquiries regarding my background. He was an old-fashioned diplomat to whom family background meant a good deal. He said he had received word that my father was a gentleman and well thought of in the United States. Dr. Guell was convinced that I would see things the correct way.

It was becoming more and more obvious to me that the Castro-led 26th of July Movement embraced every element of radical political thought and terroristic inclination in Cuba.

In early 1958 Radio Moscow openly supported the Castro revolutionaries. Early in March 1958, I notified the Department that the Cuban Army had announced the previous evening that Radio Moscow had made shortwave broadcasts asking that Castro forces be aided and abetted in overthrowing the government of Cuba. Radio Moscow throughout 1958 supported the 26th of July Movement.

In early November 1957, revolutionary organizations had formed a Unity Pact in Miami, Florida, known as the "Junta de Liberación Cubana." The 26th of July Movement was the most important revolutionary group, yet other organizations played an important role in anti-Batista activities.

Any illusions that Fidel Castro could be controlled or would co-operate with other elements of the opposition were dispelled on December 14, 1957, by a letter from Castro directed to the Junta de Liberación Cubana. This letter revealed him to be a dictatorial egomaniac. In the letter, he denounced the organization of other revolutionary groups. He denounced the Unity Pact of these groups formed in Miami, Florida. He denounced both Raúl Chibas and Dr. Felipe Pazos because they had taken it upon themselves to sign for the 26th of July Movement. He said that neither had the authority to sign for his Movement. This letter revealed Castro's intentions to install his own provisional Presidential candidate in power and his intentions to dominate the government himself.

Two of his ardent supporters, Dr. Manuel António de Varona of the Auténtico Party, and Faure Chomon, the leader of the Directório Revolucionário (Revolutionary Directorate), both denounced Castro's aims as expressed in this epistle. Some of Castro's followers in the United States, because of its contents, resigned from the Miami Unity Pact. They feared his demagogic intentions.

It was becoming clearer and clearer to those with an open mind that Cuba was torn in a struggle between a Rightist, corrupt dictator who was friendly to the United States, and a would-be Leftist dictator, who could be a Communist. As the world refused to believe Hitler in *Mein Kampf*, few heeded Castro's public announcements on various occasions prior to his landing in Oriente, in December 1956, of his socialistic plans and intentions. Most people did not want to believe his announcements. It was more popular to look upon the bearded terrorist as a crusader, even a savior.

Batista was able to remain in power because he had: (a) the support of the armed forces, (b) the support of the labor leaders, and (c) because of the general economic prosperity in the island.

Chapter VII

Censorship and Propaganda

AMERICANS IN CUBA were annoyed by the press censorship.

The following United States newspapers were circulated in Havana: the *Miami News*, the *Miami Herald*, the *New York Times* and the *Herald Tribune*. Each one would be cut out by the censors in Havana when referring to the activities of the terrorists. The news magazines, *Time* and *Newsweek*, were gone over by the scissor-employees of the Batista government. Americans in Havana, including the Embassy staff, believing in the very principle of free press, were not satisfied until all the holes in all the newspapers in Havana disappeared.

This did not take place until constitutional guarantees were reinstated.

General Cabell, Deputy Director of the Central Intelligence Agency, testified before the Internal Security Sub-Committee of the United States Senate that one of the five principal channels used by the Communists to influence Castro was "through their overt propaganda organs, radio and television commentary, and selective or false news reporting, the Communists hope to shield Fidel, and the Cuban public, from news favorable to United States policies, and to exploit news unfavorable to the United States."

By the same token, some of the liberal press in the United States became the unwitting tool of the Communist propaganda apparatus by their selective and inaccurate news reporting of events in Cuba, and by slanting the news unfavorably to the government of Cuba and favorably to Castro.

The press did much to create a popular delusion that because Batista was the dictator who unlawfully seized power, Castro must, on the other hand, represent liberty and democracy. Throughout the world, since 1917, peoples have been looking for "good leaders," "good dictators," "good governments." Usually they have permitted such persons as Stalin, Hitler, and Mussolini to rule them. Thus arose a cult of the good dictator and the bad dictator. To some, Castro looked like a good dictator before he took office.

Before Fidel Castro abandoned Cuba, he and many others of the 26th of July Movement leaders were active in the Federation of University Students (FEU), which was largely responsible for the acts of terrorism and riots in Cuba before Fidel Castro landed in the hills of Oriente in December 1956. The FEU since 1952 was a terroristic organization and was known to be infiltrated by the Communists. It had a history of involvement in common gangster activities and was under Communist influence.

When Fidel Castro was in Costa Rica, Mexico, and other places, his speeches as a student leader clearly traced a Marxist trend of political thought. Also, his interviews while in Mexico as an exile indicated the same trend of political thought.

There was a time when some in authority in the United States and some newspapermen did not want Castro to fail under any circumstances. Such persons were so fanatically bound to the revolutionary concept that they were even willing to risk the prospect of Communist control of Cuba. I do not accuse anyone of deliberately falsifying the facts, but from where I sat I could see the slanting of reports, and always the slanting was favorable to Castro.

The sympathies of the free world were for Castro, who had been portrayed by the liberal press as a Robin Hood. Every act of violence on the part of Batista was publicized on the front pages. Little mention was given to the violence of the terrorists.

In Cuban public squares, bombs were set off by the revolutionaries. Women and children were maimed. Bombs were placed by the Castro rebels in theaters, schools, stores—wherever crowds gathered. Bombing terrorists were getting bolder in Havana. This was all part of the campaign of terror to disrupt the economy of the country. Little mention of such acts of violence was made in the American press.

The American public was led to believe through false propaganda that the basic problems in Cuba were economic and social. This was not so. The basic problems were political. The best economic year in Cuba's history was 1957. For twenty-five years after President Machado's overthrow, Cuba's standard of living rose to a place among the highest in Latin America. The balance of trade favored the United States when I was Chief of Mission in Havana. Cuba bought more goods in dollars from the United States than the United States bought from Cuba, even though the United States purchased approximately 3,000,000 tons of sugar per year from Cuba with a subsidy of more than two cents per pound, which represented approximately one-half of Cuba's entire sugar production.

In 1957, Cuba's national income was 2,397,000,000 dollars.[1] The population was approximately 6,500,000.

National Income in Millions of Pesos[2]

1953	1954	1955	1956	1957	1958
1,842	1,841	1,899	2,076	2,397	2,267

The Cuban peso had been at parity with the United States dollar except for the period 1936-41. Cuba's national income was off 130 million in 1958 from the peak year 1957. Batista fled Cuba on January 1, 1959.

In July 1956, the United States Department of Commerce issued "Investment in Cuba," which said:

Subsistence living, so prevalent in many areas of Latin America, is not characteristic of Cuba, whose national income reflects the wage economy of the country. Compensation of employees represented from 56 percent to 61 percent of total national income between 1946 and 1949 and from 59 to 65 percent between 1950 and 1954.

Cuban national income has reached levels which give the Cuban people one of the highest standards of living in Latin America. The Economic and Technical mission of the International Bank for Reconstruction and Development stated in its Report on Cuba, 1951:

"The general impression of members of the Mission, from observations in travels all over Cuba, is that living levels of farmers, agricultural laborers, industrial workers, storekeepers, and others are higher all along the line than for corresponding groups in other tropical countries and in nearly all other Latin American countries.

[1] As per figures compiled by the International Monetary Fund, May 1962, Vol. XV, No. 5.
[2] *Ibid.*

This does not mean that there is no dire poverty in Cuba, but simply that in comparative terms Cubans are better off, on the average, than people of these other areas."

This statement, written in 1951, summarizes equally well the situation in 1956.

No observer with experience in Latin America can fail to be impressed by the variety, quantity, and quality of the merchandise displayed in the provincial towns and cities of the island. While such items as mechanical refrigerators, gas ranges, and television sets are prominently displayed, the strongest impressions are those formed by an inspection of stores carrying housewares, apparel and foodstuffs. Items of this nature give a more accurate clue to purchasing-power levels in Latin America than do automobile, television or refrigerator indexes.

The sugar crop, with the subsidized American quota, gave Cuba a healthy budget. A law was promulgated by the Cuban Congress when that able statesman, Dr. C. Marquez Sterling, was the presiding officer, which provided that profits were to be shared among the land owners, planters, and workers in accordance with the average sugar price. This rendered exploitation impossible.

Dr. Marquez Sterling, the leading opposition Presidential candidate in 1958, who was also the presiding officer over the Assembly which promulgated the Constitution of 1940, pointed out that:

There existed in Cuba the right of land tenure. This made it impossible for planters, tenants, joint owners, and field workers to be dispossessed even by the State itself, much less by the great monopolies which, in Cuba, as is the case even here in the United States, are always after impoverished areas. They made it necessary for Cuba, just as it was necessary for this great democracy (United States of America) to enact anti-trust legislation to regulate these rights.

Although Cuba suffered inequalities, as do all present day countries, the issues at stake during her armed struggle originated in a policy that opposed public liberties. But, as can be easily ascertained by anyone who studies the matter, the case was that, concurrent with this struggle for public power, our country was enjoying great prosperity, the year 1957 being the best in all of our history in terms of economics and finances.

Actually, as a result of the truly socio-economic revolution of 1933, the last 25 years of our existence as a republic saw Cuba attain very great heights, that in some aspects put her among the topmost ranks of the American continent.

The strong economy and the fact that Cuba enjoyed a higher standard of living than most Latin American nations was due to some extent to the close ties existing between the United States and Cuba and the influence of the large American investments in the island.

Chapter VIII

The Break Up

DURING his eighteen years as the dominant force alternately in Cuban politics, Batista had done much to keep the economy sound. He had stimulated public work programs, had obtained the aid of foreign investments, had built schools, hotels, and many highways. So many hotels were built in the nearly two years I was in Cuba in order to take care of another income source, the tourists, that the skyline of Havana began to look like a miniature Manhattan Island. Yet out in the small towns in the center of the island living conditions left much to be desired. In the small villages there was little refrigeration for the corner grocery store. The main street was often just a dirt road. Few, if any, homes had heat, and during the sudden sharp cold spells the old and the poor suffered. There was a need for low cost modern housing in the interior. Hospitals only existed miles away. Schools were transitory. Outside the Province of Havana the country was picturesque but behind the times.

Although Cuba was the last of the Latin American republics to acquire independence, a comparison of the figures shows that Cuba occupied one of the leading places in economic development.

In 1900, two years before Cuba became an independent nation, its population was approximately 1,600,000 and the country was poor. In the fifty-six years of its independence, the population grew to more than 6,500,000 and, through the free enterprise system, Cubans built a prosperous republic.

Amongst a few of the reasons for the fall of the Batista government, I might mention (obviously not complete and not listed in the order of their importance) were:

1. The day-by-day actions taken by those on the Fourth Floor of the State Department.[1]

2. The dedication to the overthrow of all Rightist Dictators by certain influential persons and institutions in the United States.

3. Dishonesty and corruption which brought about disintegration within the government of Cuba and permeated down through the armed services.

4. Strong-arm methods of law enforcement agencies.

5. The need for honest, free and open elections.

6. Lack of education for the masses.

7. The need for schools and hospitals in the outside provinces.

8. The need for low-cost housing in the interior.

9. Diversification of the economy—Cuba was too dependent

[1] Reference to the Fourth Floor of the State Department must be taken symbolically. The Fourth Floor is where the officials dealing with Latin American Affairs have their offices.

on one product, sugar. The entire economy of the country was based on the volume and value of the sugar crop. The volume affected employment, length of the Zafra (sugar-making season), railway traffic and port movement. The value of the sugar crop determined wage levels and the amount of money in circulation. During the sugar season there was prosperity in the interior of the island. During the dead season of the sugar harvest, the Batista government created employment for the workers through deficit spending. Attempts were made to rectify Cuba's dependence on the cultivation of sugar cane by diversifying its agricultural production, developing the mining industry and developing the cattle and dairy industry.

On August 30, 1960, the following colloquy took place on "The Fall of Batista" at the United States Senate Sub-Committee Hearings:

Senator Eastland: Did Castro ever win a battle?

Mr. Smith: Castro never won a military victory. The best victories that Castro ever won were raids upon Cuban guardhouses that are spread out through the hinterland and small skirmishes with government troops.

Senator Eastland: How did he come to power? First, why did Batista leave?

Mr. Smith: Why did Batista leave?

Senator Eastland: Yes.

Mr. Smith: If the United States had been completely impartial, in my opinion, Batista would not have had to leave Cuba until after the inauguration of the president-elect (Rivero Aguero).

Senator Eastland: He didn't have to leave. He had not been defeated by armed force.

Mr. Smith: Let me put it to you this way: that there are a lot of reasons for Batista's moving out. Batista had been in control off and on for [eighteen] years. His government was disintegrating, at the end, due to corruption [and] to the fact that he had been in power too long. Police brutality was getting worse.

I further testified:

The fact that the United States was no longer supporting Batista had a devastating psychological effect upon the armed forces and upon the leaders of the labor movement. This went a long way toward bringing about his downfall.

On the other hand, our actions in the United States were responsible for the rise to power of Castro. Until certain portions of the American press began to write derogatory articles against the Batista government, the Castro revolution never got off first base.

Batista made the mistake of overemphasizing the importance of [Dr. Carlos] Prio [Socarras], who was residing in Florida, and underestimating the importance of Castro. Prio was operating out of the United States, out of Florida, supplying the revolutionaries with arms, ammunition, bodies and money.

Batista told me that when Prio left Cuba, Prio and Alameia took $140 million out of Cuba. If we cut that estimate in half, they may have shared $70 million. It is believed that Prio spent a great many millions of dollars in the United States assisting the revolutionaries. This was done right from our shores.

Senator Eastland: No effort was made to stop it?

Mr. Smith: The Batista government complained continually about the airlifts and airdrops of bodies and arms from the United States. I always kept the State Department fully informed.

But we seemed to have great trouble in enforcing our neutrality laws. I have sometimes wished that we had been half as diligent at that time in enforcing our neutrality laws as we have been lately.

As American Ambassador it was easy to see the handwriting on the wall—that Cuba had to have a new leader, one who believed in the democratic processes of government for the people, but it was also obvious that Castro was not the answer. It was so apparent to me from my first-hand reports on Castro that he was not the answer that, as I stated in a press conference at Washington on January 16, 1958, one year before Batista fled Cuba, "The United States would never be able to do business with Fidel Castro."

I knew by that time that Fidel Castro should never be the ruler of Cuba. His record was one of a gun-toting terrorist who hired himself out to revolutionary forces who wanted to unseat governments in Latin America. Whether or not Castro was a card-bearing Communist when he first landed in Oriente was not the main issue. The important points were: his record of emotional instability, radical socialist political thinking plus a deep-seated hatred for the United States, and, outside of Cuba, the police record of a violent terrorist.

Under oath before the Senate Sub-Committee, I testified August 1960:

The Communists are too smart to infiltrate too openly at the beginning and disclose their hand. Many times when I was in Cuba I said that the 26th of July Movement, the revolutionary movement, was a Boy Scout movement compared to the Communists, and that the Communists would apply the blotting paper to the 26th of July Movement as they saw fit, and they did sop it up as they saw fit.

By no longer openly supporting the existing government of Cuba, the United States helped Castro rise to power in preference to a number of politically sound and friendly leaders we might have supported. The nuances behind our then lagging and diffident support of Batista had a devastating psychological effect on the armed forces and the leaders of the labor movement. These leaders became nervous and frightened. The regime began to disintegrate from within. The rumor of no further support from the United States for Batista spread, but until some idealistic but unrealistic members of the American press descended on Cuba to destroy Batista and create a world-wide picture of the new savior of the people, Fidel Castro, the Castro revolution never got off the ground.

It was unfortunate that so many of the American press who came to Cuba did not visit the American Embassy to discuss the United States stand on Cuba and Castro. It is the duty of reporters to write the facts as objectively as possible. In some cases, before they returned home to write their opinions of a complicated situation, they spent only twenty-four hours in Cuba, which is hardly enough to obtain more than a glimpse of the country. At one point, we even had an influx of TV personalities who became authorities and over-night sages.

Take the example of Mr. Jack Paar, who came to Cuba to spend a few days producing a Cuban version of his nighttime variety show. The producer invited my wife and me to appear in the audience at the Tropicana so the cameras could briefly photograph us. Since I do not approve of superficial publicity, I refused, and fortunately so, for Mr. Paar returned to America as one of Castro's prominent admirers.

There was one newspaperman brave enough to announce in print that he had made a mistake in judgment, and I refer to Mr. Ed Sullivan. After a short visit in Cuba, he wrote:

United States Ambassador to Cuba, Earl E. T. Smith, and his staff missed the boat completely. They swallowed Batista's propaganda, hook, line and sinker. In Sunday's papers, the White House announced that Ambassador Smith's resignation had been accepted. Our Ambassador should have listened to veteran American foreign correspondents in Latin America. *Chicago Trib's* Jules Dubois begged Ambassador Smith not to allow the United States Military Commission to train Batista's fliers for bombing forays against the people of Cuba, pointing out that Castro's bearded army represented and was expressing the deep feeling of the people of Cuba. Our Embassy in Havana ridiculed this interpretation, gave the green light to Batista's bombing of the populace. If our State Department would instruct the United States Embassy biggies all over the world to contact American foreign correspondents on the scene, get the benefit of their man-in-the-street savvy, we would be spared incidents such as the fiasco in Cuba.[2]

[2] *New York Daily News,* January 12, 1959.

The Break Up

It took courage when, on April 4, 1960, Sullivan wrote further:

Earl E. T. Smith, former Ambassador to Cuba, relieved from that post when Castro came to power, hasn't been congratulated for his analysis of Castro by any of us who rapped him at the time. But Smith was right and everybody else was wrong.[3]

Too many people, without thoughtful consideration and without diligent study of the facts, reach fixed conclusions about complex political and economic situations of a nation in a day or two. This is unfortunately true not only of tourists but also of newspapermen and television commentators. Granted that Batista had outserved his usefulness, those who so flippantly decided in favor of Castro imperiled not only Cuba but also the United States.

[3] *New York Daily News,* April 4, 1960.

Chapter IX

Assassination and Confidence

IN DECEMBER 1957, about six months after my arrival, the American Embassy in Havana was informed that Communist members of the Castro revolution were plotting my assassination for political reasons. Information of the plot came to us from intelligence sources at the American Embassy at Ciudad Trujillo, Dominican Republic. The plot, which was later verified by the State Department, called for two Communists to be sent to Havana from Mexico City to kill the American Ambassador. The plan was to create an international incident in the hope that the resultant scandal would bring about the fall of the Batista government.

Intelligence sources of the Haitian Embassy in Mexico City also learned of the Communist murder plot. The Haitian Army Attaché in Cuba notified the United States Army Attaché, Lieutenant Colonel Joseph Treadway, of the reports received by the Haitian Embassy. Although the subject of protection was discussed and bodyguards were offered, they were neither wanted nor did I accept them. Accepting bodyguards would have offended the better elements of the opposition.

Our only concern was for the safety of our five-year-old son. Because of the possibility of kidnaping, I arranged to have a Cuban employee of the Embassy accompany the boy on his way to and from school.

While I was in Washington on one of my trips for consultation, the situation in Havana was particularly tense due to the stepped-up terroristic activities of the revolutionaries and the increased repressive measures of the police. I believed it necessary to contact my wife, Florence, to remind her discreetly that our son was ill and that he should remain within the Embassy residence according to doctor's orders. It was necessary to disguise our conversation, as all the Embassy telephones were tapped by the Batista government. Florence understood immediately. She reassured me by saying that she planned to keep little Earl in his bedroom because he was coming down with a cold.

On January 24, 1958, Batista appealed for an electoral solution and publicly promised to turn the government over to his duly elected successor. Yet Batista certainly did not help his cause with the Department or with the Embassy by having a law passed which would make him eligible to command the military in the ensuing administration. According to this legislation, Batista would be eligible to assume the new position of Chairman of the Joint Chiefs of Staff. The opposition immediately asserted that Batista intended to perpetuate himself in office.

It was the desire of the revolutionaries to destroy the confidence of the people in the government of Cuba and to disrupt the economy of Cuba. In 1957 and in early 1958, these activities on the part of the revolutionaries had little effect.

It was not until the early summer of 1958 that such stepped-up activities began to have an effect on the economy of Cuba. For a time, the Castro revolutionaries acted more like irresponsible hoodlums than like a well-directed organization. By the fall of 1958, the revolutionaries appeared to be receiving professional advice on how to disrupt the economy of Cuba; i.e., destroying the main arteries of transportation by blowing up bridges and dislocating principal highways, blowing up railroad tracks, and attacking railroad trains. As a result of the disruption of transportation, widespread fear prevailed in the island regarding the ability to transport the sugar harvest to the mills. Communications were disrupted by destroying telephone and telegraph lines. The revolutionaries were attempting to cut the island in half at Las Villas Province by shutting off all transportation and communication between the two ends of the island. The change from casual attacks to a well-directed campaign was surprising.

The rebels made periodic raids on the Nicaro Nickel Mine, owned by the United States Government and the Moa Bay Nickel Mine, owned by the Freeport Sulphur Company. In response to my request Batista sent troops to both nickel mines to protect these properties. He said to me: "I will place 1,000 men at each mine, if you will supply me with 2,000 rifles."

Batista always tried to be co-operative and always tried to accede to the Embassy requests, especially for the protection and saving of American lives. Batista insisted that he was conscious of his responsibility for the preservation of law and order, including the saving of American lives and the protection of American property, although there was boiling trouble underneath. Batista did not want it said that his government was no longer able to live up to such responsibilities. I cannot recall any time when he did not make an effort to live up to the responsibility of protection of American lives and property.

Batista would say to me: "You come to me for the saving of American lives and the protection of American property. This is the responsibility of the government of Cuba which I shall live up to. Yet I cannot understand why your government refuses to sell arms to my government which is friendly to you and an enemy of Communism." I can well recall him asking me, "Can you name another friendly government to whom you will not sell arms?"

Whenever I asked President Batista for Cuba's vote to support the United States in the United Nations, he would instruct his Foreign Minister to have the Cuban delegation vote in accordance with the United States delegation and to give full support to the American delegation at the United Nations.

My prediction at the first Embassy staff meeting that "the job of American Ambassador to Havana during that period was a post at which no Ambassador could win" was being proven correct. For to be correct, the American Ambassador should be strictly impartial and as I said at the staff meeting, "I know Cubans well enough to know that you must be either with them or against them."

The United States was receiving caustic criticism from both sides of the fight. Our alleged policy was complete non-intervention. Yet antagonistic forces in Cuba assailed us despite our impartial position in the long-simmering revolt.

The rebels stated that our non-intervention tended to favor the Batista regime because the government in power enjoyed official recognition by the United States. This fact promoted anti-American feeling among the rebels because it tended to work against them.

On the other hand, government officials were deeply upset because the State Department suspended the shipments of arms to the government of Cuba. Officials of the Batista regime were upset because we did not enforce our neutrality laws; because we were permitting news releases about the government of Cuba to be slanted—playing up government of Cuba atrocities and playing down rebel atrocities; and because of our "intervention by innuendo"—using moral pressure to block the sale of arms to the government of Cuba by other powers.

Before the suspension of sale of arms, American military aid was supplied to Batista for hemisphere defense as a protection against "any Communist subversion," and we were getting more and more evidence that the 26th of July Movement under Fidel Castro was being infiltrated by Communists and becoming more and more Communist-controlled.

At the same time, the revolutionaries were irate with the United States because they believed that it was American-made planes and American-made bombs (previously delivered to the government of Cuba) that were dropped on the city of Cienfuegos during the Naval uprising in September 1957. Also the revolutionaries were furious with the United States and with the American Ambassador because American arms were allegedly being used by Batista forces against the revolutionaries in Oriente Province. Such arms had been supplied to the Cuban government under the Military Defense Assistance Program.

The proclaimed policy of the United States was non-intervention—although for a power as great as the United States, it is nearly impossible not to intervene in a country as closely associated with us as Cuba had been. Before Castro, Cuban-American relations were warm, close and friendly. For years we had been together in a common fight against Communist subversion. The Cubans and ourselves had fought side by side on several occasions in defense of democratic ideals. Before Castro, Cuba was as loyal and had been as good a friend of the United States as any of our sister nations. Both the government of Cuba and the 26th of July Movement expected us to help them and expected us not to help the other side.

Chapter X

Washington Press Conference

IT HAD BECOME OBVIOUS to me but not to William Wieland, Director of the Office of Caribbean and Mexican Affairs of the State Department (MID Section), that Fidel Castro was not the solution for Cuba's political problems. In early January 1958, Wieland visited the American Embassy in Havana and showed us a paper he had written, which depicted the economy of Cuba as crumbling and recommended that the United States apply pressure on the government of Cuba to hasten its downfall. Actually, economic conditions in Cuba had never been better than in the year which had just ended. His paper went on to say that the government of Cuba would probably fall in a relatively short period of time.

The purpose of his visit to Havana was to have the Embassy prepare and submit a paper along the same lines, endorsing his stand. William Wieland and John Topping, head of the Embassy's political division, prepared for the Embassy an outline of such a paper, depicting a poor economy in Cuba under chaotic conditions and anticipating the early fall of the government of Cuba.

When this paper was brought to my attention, I disagreed with the premise. I went on to say that any paper that Wieland wished to prepare along such lines could be sent to the State Department only over his own signature. Any paper that left the Embassy over my signature would be along very different lines.

Because of Wieland's visit to Havana, I decided to go to Washington to explain in person my thoughts on the political problems of Cuba. So I telephoned Assistant Secretary Roy Rubottom, stating that I wished to go to Washington for consultation and was prepared to debate the economic and political situation of Cuba with anyone. Mr. Rubottom said that the Department did not have sufficient funds left to pay for my trip. I countered by saying that I would be happy to pay my own expenses. He then agreed to have me come up and arranged for the necessary travel orders to be issued.

I arrived in Washington on January 16 and was met at the railroad terminal by Mr. Wieland and Mr. Leonhardy (Cuban Desk Officer). Mr. Wieland informed me that he had arranged a press conference for that afternoon at two-thirty. I objected to the press conference, as I had nothing of interest which I could disclose to the press. Wieland said that it was too late to cancel.

At a consultation that morning in Secretary Rubottom's office, I informed the State Department officers that Batista had agreed to lift the press censorship and would restore constitutional guarantees. However, this information was not to be leaked, as President Batista would not make the announcement for several days. Mr. Wieland's paper was not discussed again between us and was discarded on Secretary Rubottom's instructions.

In return for the restoration of constitutional guarantees I was authorized to inform Batista that he could expect delivery of the twenty armored cars which had been on order for nine months. At the same time, I was asked by the State Department to inform Batista that it was the United States' hope that he would be able to eliminate violence in the country and could create conditions which would be acceptable for free and open elections.

After attending a press conference of the Secretary of State, John Foster Dulles, on January 16, during lunch hour, I hurried to Mr. Wieland's office where I found Mr. Leonhardy, as well as Mr. Wieland, and members of the press. I read the prepared statement which said that the United States hoped the government of Cuba would hold acceptable elections, spoke of our concern with the political problems of Cuba, and reiterated our intentions strictly to adhere to our policy of non-intervention.

After reading the statement, I was asked, off the record, whether I thought the United States government would be able to do business with Fidel Castro. My reply was that I did not believe the United States would ever be able to do business with Fidel Castro. Then I was asked the reasons for my statement. I replied that the United States Government can only do business with a government that will honor its international obligations and that can maintain law and order. In my opinion, Castro would do neither.

Although the statement was made off the record, within twenty-four hours Castro, in the Sierra Maestra, and certain pro-Castro members of the United States Congress, had received word that I had stated that Fidel Castro was a Communist, although my statement was as printed above. From that time on (nearly twelve months before Batista fled), I was officially on record as being against Castro. Also, from that time on, the revolutionaries and the Communists carried on a campaign to destroy my effectiveness. The leak to Castro of my off-the-record statement could only have come from someone in the State Department or from one of the newspapermen present. It was also leaked that the government of Cuba intended to restore constitutional guarantees.

When I returned to Havana I was met by reporters. I realized the government of Cuba would be annoyed at the premature public disclosure of its intention to restore guarantees at the expiration of the current period of suspension, on January 29, 1958. So I made the following factual statement, hoping to pour oil on the troubled waters: "I wish that business in general in the United States was as flourishing as it is in Cuba." At that time, we were in a recession in the United States.

The next day, January 17, the Cuban press carried front-page stories of the prepared release, with emphasis on the non-intervention aspect of the statement. No mention was made of my remarks about Fidel Castro. These remarks had been off the record. Minister of the Interior, Santiago Rey, speaking for the government, indicated the government's annoyance at the premature public disclosure of its intentions to restore guarantees by saying that constitutional guarantees would be restored "as rapidly as possible and when circumstances so advised"; that he was touched by the State Department's concern regarding the internal matters of Cuba and that he realized good friends may be concerned with each other's problems; that the government of Cuba was appreciative of the American concern in the forthcoming elections; and that the government of Cuba realized that the Ambassador also meant to call upon agitators and terrorists in Cuba to desist in their campaign of terrorism at the time the Ambassador expressed hope that constitutional guarantees would be restored.

However, Santiago Rey's statement did not alter the government of Cuba's intentions to restore guarantees at the expiration of the current period of suspension on January 29. On January 18, Dr. Guell reiterated, in confidence, that guarantees would be restored at the end of the month, subject to no unforeseen violence erupting.

Encounters between the Army and rebel forces continued. The pro-Castro American press played up the rebel attacks. According to rebel reports various towns would be captured and occupied by the rebels. However, such towns could be held for only a few hours. The rebels would withdraw before the Army arrived. The American press built up the rebel reports and discounted the official reports that government troops had suffered no casualties in their encounters with rebel forces. Pro-Castro press circles referred to the Cuban Army as the "bullet-proof army."

On January 20, 1958, the six-man Cuban delegation representing the Confederation of Cuban Workers (CTC) returned from an executive committee meeting of the Inter-American Regional Organization of Workers (ORIT) held in Washington from January 13-15, 1958. The CTC secretary, Eusebio Mujal, reported that the ORIT executive committee had unanimously agreed to declare that it had absolute confidence that the guarantees set by the Cuban Government and the legislative power for the elections would be complied with and that this would carry the country along the road to democracy, peace, and liberty.

With the support of the armed services and the labor leaders, plus a boom economy, the government of Cuba appeared for the time being safely entrenched at the beginning of 1958.

Chapter XI

Broken Promises and Deceptions

THE EMBASSY had been receiving reports of the maltreatment of various 26th of July leaders, who were being held in the Santiago jail. They were: Antonio Buch, Javier Pazos, Armando Hart, and Emilio Vallejo. As a result of the interest shown by the Embassy, and because of press reports, on January 18 newsmen in Santiago were permitted to visit the revolutionary leaders. General Alberto del Rio Chaviano, Commander-in-Chief of the Armed Forces of Oriente Province, explained that the purpose of the invitation for the newsmen to visit the revolutionary leaders was to disprove accounts in the American press that they had been tortured or killed. Newsmen reported that the prisoners appeared to be in good physical condition. The Embassy received reports from Intelligence sources that the mothers of Antonio Buch and Armando Hart were permitted to visit their sons. Despite this incident stories of police brutalities still persisted.

Shortly after my return to Cuba, I informed President Batista that he would receive delivery of the armored cars. I then said, "Mr. President, may I make a suggestion and ask that you will not consider it as intervening in the affairs of your country?"

President Batista replied, "You are at liberty to say anything you want, Mr. Ambassador."

I pointed out that his public relations in the United States were extremely poor and I suggested that it would create a favorable reaction in the United States if he were able to remove some of the police officials who had been accused of excessive violence. The President told me that he agreed, but that it would be very difficult for him to take such action as it would be interpreted as a sign of weakness. Batista had a tiger by the tail. In accordance with my consultations at the Department, I further suggested to Batista that he try to create an appropriate atmosphere for general elections, and that he should declare a general amnesty for political prisoners.

President Batista agreed with these suggestions and referred to them in a speech which he made before a political gathering. At the same time, he announced his intention to end the suspension of constitutional guarantees in all but Oriente Province, and to lift the press censorship, which was done on January 25, 1958.

However, the State Department later failed to live up to its promise to deliver the twenty armored cars.

Since the previous fall, I had made every effort during many meetings with Batista to obtain the restoration of constitutional guarantees and the lifting of the press censorship. Batista had finally agreed, although he was complaining bitterly about United States failure to enforce its neutrality laws.

Bodies, ammunition, and arms were being shipped in a steady stream from Florida and were being delivered to the revolutionaries in the hills of the Sierra Maestra.

Finally, due to the efforts of our able Assistant Attorney General William F. Tompkins, the Justice Department obtained an indictment by the Federal Grand Jury in February 1958 against Dr. Prio Socarras, former President of Cuba, who had been the main source of shipment of contraband arms from Florida to the revolutionists. Agents of Prio were the biggest offenders and for some time they openly defied United States neutrality laws by shipping matériel from Florida to the revolutionary forces in the Sierra Maestra and the Sierra del Escambray.

In addition to Dr. Prio and his agents there were many active groups operating in the United States to bring about the downfall of the Batista government.

The Civic Resistance Movement, an organization formed in Santiago de Cuba to aid and abet the 26th of July Movement, was operating in the United States. Among other groups operating in the United States were the Workers Universal, the Democratic Party, Fourth of April Organization, and the Party of the Cuban People.

On February 19, 1958, at a meeting with the President of the Republic, I suggested that he invite representatives of (a) the United Nations, (b) the Organization of American States, and (c) the world press to witness the elections. Batista was receptive but indicated that the timing for such a move was very important. At the moment, he said, the government was occupied with the filing of political slates.

Some of the middle-of-the-road press in Cuba endorsed the elections and stated that the ballot box would be the only solution to the problem. The newspaper *Prensa Libre* urged both sides to arrive at a peaceful solution. *El Mundo,* whose publisher was anti-Batista, stated in an editorial at the end of January 1958, "The basic problem for Cuba of re-establishing institutional normality should be solved at the ballot box in a climate of absolute guarantees for all. With the re-establishment of constitutional guarantees and the lifting of censorship, the government has taken an important step toward making elections feasible. If a free climate is established as the government has promised, it is the duty of the opposition to mobilize civically to the ballot box."

Fidel Castro was violently opposed to elections and announced that anyone, including the political opponents of Batista who participated in general elections, would be imprisoned or killed by the revolutionaries.

By December 1957, it was becoming more and more clear that the only way to salvage the situation was eventually to have Batista relinquish the Presidency and concurrently appoint a broadly based national unity government without Castro and without representatives of the terrorists, but including representatives of the better elements of the opposition. The mandate of such a broadly based national unity government would only be in effect until general elections had been held.

I had an exchange of views with this in mind with Cuban civic leaders, among them being Dr. Guillermo Belt, former Ambassador from Cuba to the United States. He was very knowledgeable about Castro and was in touch with many prominent Cubans who would be willing to serve in a broadly based national unity government. However, the co-operation of none of these individuals could be obtained without the support of the United States, as no such plan could be effective without our support.

Luis Machado, former Cuban Ambassador to the United

States, was also very active in attempting the formation of another peace committee, which was never formed.

Guillermo Belt was anti-Batista but had good reason to fear Castro much more. Dr. Belt was Cuba's representative at the Ninth Inter-American Conference that convened in Bogotá, March 30-May 2, 1948, at the time of the "Bogotazo," which occurred on April 9, 1948. The "Bogotazo" of 1948 started with the assassination of Jorge Eliecer Gaitan, Liberal leader, so as to provoke the uprising of the masses that comprised the Liberal party, since Gaitan enjoyed immense popularity. The Bogotá uprising was Communist-inspired and Communist-controlled, by a key group of international Communist leaders and activists who were brought to Bogotá for that purpose. The effort to shatter the Ninth Inter-American Conference at Bogotá and to demonstrate to the world the power of the Communist-led mob to spread havoc was part of the general anti-United States strategy.[1]

At the Bogotá uprising, Fidel Castro played his first serious role as an active organizer of Communist insurrection. He was then twenty-two years old and a student at Havana University Law School. It was Dr. Guillermo Belt who gave asylum to Fidel Castro in the Cuban Embassy and arranged for his safe conduct to Cuba after the Bogotá uprising. Dr. Belt told me Fidel Castro was accused of committing several murders at the Bogotá uprising.

When I asked Dr. Belt why he had given asylum to Castro in the Cuban Embassy and why he had arranged for Castro's safe conduct to Cuba, he replied he was unaware at the time of Castro's crimes.

The Department of State must have been fully informed not only of Fidel Castro's police record but also of his active participation in the Communist-inspired and Communist-

[1] Nathaniel Weyl gives an authentic account of the Bogotá uprising in *Red Star over Cuba.*

controlled uprising in Bogotá. Yet, no one in the State Department ever mentioned the Bogotá uprising to me during the briefing period in the State Department when I was being prepared to assume my new post as Chief of Mission in Havana. I cannot recall anyone making a derogatory remark regarding Fidel Castro during that time, although Mr. Rubottom and Mr. Wieland arranged to have me briefed on Castro's virtues by Herbert Matthews, whom they accepted as an expert. I can never recall during my briefing or while I was Chief of Mission in Havana any expression of approval from the Fourth Floor of the friendly government of Cuba.

My first information of Castro's part in the Bogotá uprising came from Dr. Belt, months after I had assumed my post as Chief of Mission in Havana. I was not told that Assistant Secretary of State for Latin American affairs, Roy Rubottom, at the time of the Bogotá uprising, was in Bogotá, Colombia, serving as Secretary and Consul in the American Embassy from 1947-1949.[2] Secretary Rubottom also served as Secretary to the United States Delegation, Ninth International Conference of American States, Bogotá, Colombia, 1948.[3] I was not aware of this fact until after I testified before the Senate Committee.

Fidel Castro was a member of the Communist group aimed at wrecking the organization to which Secretary Rubottom served as Secretary (Ninth International Conference of American States).

To return to my conversations with the Cuban civic leaders, none of them would dare risk incurring the wrath of both the Batista government and Fidel Castro unless a peace plan had a chance of success. They knew they could not succeed without the support of the United States. A national unity government would only act as a provisional government and

[2] Listed in *Who's Who in America*, Vol. 28.
[3] *Ibid.*

would remain in office only long enough to hold general elections.

I had many meetings with the Papal Nuncio, Monsignor Luigi Centoz, for an exchange of views along these lines. The Papal Nuncio, a charming, elderly gentleman with keen, piercing blue eyes, had very little knowledge of English. In spite of my lessons, my Spanish was still very poor. Therefore, our conversations were carried on in French.

It was the hope of the Papal Nuncio that a bridge could be established between Castro and Batista. In the words of the Papal Nuncio: "Pour etablir un pont entre Batista et Castro." However, he agreed that peace should be sought through a national unity government.

When the Papal Nuncio asked if the United States Government would lend its support to our plans, I regretted to say that I was unable to get any committment from the State Department. The State Department would not permit me to give any indications of support to the Roman Catholic Church. The position of the State Department was that only if the efforts of the Church were proven successful would the United States issue any public statement of endorsement. To do otherwise would be considered intervention.

It was my understanding with the Papal Nuncio that the national unity government would include members of the political opposition, representatives of the revolutionaries, and members of the government of Cuba—representatives of all segments. It was to be a broadly-based government and Batista was to preside. Although the hierarchy of the Church took the position that peace should be obtained through a national unity government, not all of the Roman Catholic Church took the same position. There was discord among members of the Church. The Acción Católica and the JOC (Young Catholic Workers) were hoping for the fall of Batista and were sympathetic to Castro.

(69)

While I was representing the United States in Cuba, Castro's representatives were receiving a sympathetic ear on the Fourth Floor of the State Department.

In July of 1958, at a conference in Caracas, Venezuela, a confederation was formed of the revolutionary groups, known as the Civic Revolutionary Front. Dr. José Miro Cardona, a political exile, acted as secretary of this association. He told me that he had become a very good friend of William Wieland of our State Department.

In addition to the legally established representative of the revolutionaries, Ernesto Betancourt, the State Department established a liaison with the revolutionaries through Dr. Miro Cardona, former Dean of the Cuban Bar Association. Dr. Miro Cardona, a Fidelista, was strongly opposed to any solution that did not turn the government of Cuba over to Castro. Despite their dealings with the representatives of the revolutionaries, the State Department maintained that it was not intervening in Cuban affairs.

At the end of January Fidel Castro was in a conciliatory mood. He sent a proposal to Batista to end Cuba's civil war. It was reported that Castro would agree to general elections under President Batista, provided the elections were supervised throughout the island by the Organization of American States, and provided Batista would agree to the withdrawal of all government military forces from Oriente Province. Castro also wanted the Army to leave behind all equipment, as the rebels were in dire need of equipment.

In an exclusive interview with Homer Bigart of the *New York Times*, Castro explained why he wanted to have military control of Oriente as a precondition to elections. "With his own troops guarding Oriente polls and with foreign observers liberally scattered throughout all Provinces, Senor Castro believes that his 26th of July Movement would sweep the election."

The *New York Times* editorial writer went on to say that Senor Castro's proposal was submitted to Congressman Manuel de Jesús León Ramirez of Manzanillo on January 28 and that the representative later conferred with members of the Batista Cabinet.

Rumors of Castro's offer leaked out in Havana. Although Batista most likely would not accept Castro's demand for evacuation of Oriente, he had personally assured me that he would agree to OAS observers witnessing the general elections. Here was an opportunity for the United States, with the aid of the Church, to establish a "bridge between Castro and Batista."

In early February, the rebel strength was at a low ebb and Castro was much more conciliatory. He was concerned that he might be losing the sympathetic support of the United States, because of the arrest in Miami of Dr. Carlos Prio Socarras for having violated United States neutrality laws.

Were the State Department willing, this was an opportune time for me to approach Batista about absenting himself from Cuba and appointing a broadly-based national unity government excluding Castro. On the grounds of non-intervention, the State Department never seriously explored any suggested plan for a peaceful solution that would exclude Castro. Therefore, the Cuban political situation could only further decline.

Castro publicly insinuated that a deal had been made between the United States and the Cuban government. According to Castro, Batista had been prevailed upon to restore constitutional guarantees in return for United States agreement to take action against Cuban revolutionary groups in the United States who were shipping arms and money to the Sierra.

In the latter part of February 1958, the Roman Catholic Church of Cuba came to the decision to mediate in the political affairs of Cuba by itself. It was originally planned that a committee should be appointed with representatives of the Church, labor, the universities, civic organizations, and the press. Such a committee would first visit the President. This was good news at the time because in this way a peaceful solution might be obtained. The people of Cuba, who were now tiring of the revolution, were greatly encouraged by the possibility of a peaceful solution through the Church.

On the first of March, 1958, the hierarchy of the Roman Catholic Church in Cuba, under the leadership of the Cardinal and the Papal Nuncio, took a definite stand by releasing a statement which called on the revolutionaries of Cuba to desist from their terroristic activities, and called on the government of Cuba to bring about a peaceful solution through the formation of a national unity government. The statement, which was signed by the Church hierarchy, did not go into details as to what groups should be included in the national unity government. In reply to my question, the Papal Nuncio said the Church had in mind leaders of the opposition group, but not Fidel Castro.

Chapter XII

The Election and Intervention

ON THE MORNING of March 3, 1958, Dr. Gonzalo Guell asked me to stop at his house on the way to the Chancellery. When I arrived, he informed me that the President had agreed to my requests (a) to invite the world press to witness elections, (b) to invite observers from the United Nations to witness the elections, and (c) to invite representatives of the OAS to witness the elections. He added that the President of Cuba was prepared to co-operate in every way possible to create a favorable atmosphere for elections, and would guarantee free

and open elections. It seemed that the actions of the Church had hastened Batista's decision.

The final decision by the Church was to name a small committee which would not be considered hostile to Batista. It was also feared that a large committee would be too unwieldly, so on March 6, 1958, from the Cardinal's Palace it was announced that a National Unity Committee would be formed in the hope that a peaceful solution could be found to the political problems of Cuba. The members of the Committee were as follows: Raúl de Cardenas, ex-Vice-President of Cuba; Gustavo Cuervo Rubio, ex-Vice-President of Cuba; Pastor Gonzales, representative of the Church; Victor Pedroso, President of the Cuban Bankers' Association.

The Committee was well received in Cuba, for hope still prevailed for a peaceful solution. Editorials in the Cuban press strongly endorsed the Church's stand that peace should be sought through a national unity government. Leading newspapers published the suggestions of the Peace Committee which called for the following actions to create a climate favorable for elections:

(a) Political amnesty.
(b) All exiles to return to Cuba.
(c) Constitutional guarantees be re-established.
(d) Members of the 26th of July Movement be permitted to take part in the elections.

Bearing in mind that Batista and Fidel Castro were the only important factors, the National Unity Committee, which came to be known as the National Harmony Commission, originally planned to solicit the support of the press, universities, civic organizations, labor, and the political opposition. After such support had been obtained, the plan was that the Harmony Commission would approach the revolutionaries, and seek their co-operation for a peaceful solution. Even if

(74)

the revolutionaries would not co-operate, then these groups were to continue to negotiate with the government. However, the Commission first met with Batista. After several days the President received the National Harmony Commission and informed them that he was willing to co-operate with their suggestion of forming a National Unity government, but that he would not shorten his mandate. He would not relinquish the Presidency before it legally expired on February 24, 1959.

The President released the following public statement:

(A) Although the Government of Cuba had always considered that all outside observers witnessing a Cuban election would be considered as intervening in the affairs of Cuba, he was prepared to invite the United Nations to send observers and he was prepared to invite the world press to observe the elections, if the opposition so requested.

(B) He was willing to co-operate with any of the demands of the opposition to create a favorable atmosphere for elections.

Batista, at this time, was in the process of selecting a new Cabinet. To make a conciliatory offer he appointed several professional people and appointed Núñez Portuondo as Prime Minister. Batista selected Núñez Portuondo because he was well regarded in the United States and at the United Nations.

Under the guidance of the Church the Commission made overtures to Fidel Castro. However, the Harmony Commission was rebuffed by Castro because he believed the Commission was too pro-Batista and it did not have the support of the United States. He not only refused to receive the Commission but would not receive any of its representatives. This occurred on March 10, 1958. Castro said the Cabinet would not be acceptable to him if Batista presided. As a result, the entire Cabinet resigned. Foreign Minister Gonzalo Guell was appointed Prime Minister and held both offices until Batista fled.

Batista, the "strong man," had been willing to mediate—

but not Fidel. As a result, Castro became the man of the hour and his prestige grew, while Batista's declined because his willingness to mediate was interpreted as a sign of weakness.

The National Harmony Commission now had no choice but to resign after Fidel Castro rejected their peace offer. Such action was taken on March 12 and the hope was expressed that their objectives would be obtained through the formation of another committee.

From the Papal Nuncio I learned that the Church did intend to appoint a new committee of three Bishops: one from Matanzas, Bishop Martin Villaverde; one from Oriente Province, Archbishop Perez Serantes; and one from Las Villas Province, Archbishop Dalmau. The Church was aware that if the government of Cuba fell, it would be blamed by the government supporters for having intervened. Nevertheless, the Church was anxious for humanitarian reasons to find a peaceful solution.

The Cuban Episcopacy hoped that the Archbishop, Perez Serantes, would still have influence on Fidel Castro, because in 1953, he had saved Fidel's life by arranging his safe delivery to the civil courts in Oriente after the attack on the Moncada barracks. The Church was bitterly disappointed that Castro had rejected the peace offers of the National Harmony Commission and finally decided for the time being to adopt a waiting policy. This I learned on March 10 when I visited the Papal Nuncio at his residence.

After January 25, 1958, when constitutional guarantees were restored, the terrorists stepped up their activities. Bombs were placed in movie houses, theaters, stores, and in public squares. Young girls carried the bombs into movie houses under their skirts. Some of them were badly hurt when the bombs exploded too soon. There was widespread violence. The burning of the sugar cane, to harm the economy of Cuba, was intensified. Rats and mice were released, with burning rags tied on their tails, to run through the cane fields.

Such acts as high-jacking commercial aircraft were stepped up to show the world that the government of Cuba could not maintain law and order. The Argentine racing driver, Juan Fangio, was kidnaped to obtain publicity.

In the Church's and my attempts to find a solution we were receiving moral support through many civic organizations which were alarmed because of the terroristic activities of the revolutionaries. Peace was desired by most people, including the better elements of the opposition. The terroristic revolutionaries and ardent supporters of Fidel Castro did not want general elections. They feared any such attempt which would bring about general elections and which would set up a provisional government in Cuba with Batista out of the country. If Batista removed himself from office and left Cuba, the primary objective which Fidel Castro allegedly was fighting for would be obtained—namely, to remove the despot. Castro then would have no bona fide cause to continue the revolution.

During this period many civic organizations, as well as professional and religious organizations, believed that elections were desirable but could not be held unless tranquillity was restored to the country.

On March 10 all the schools in Cuba were closed. Fear was spreading throughout the island. Acts of terrorism and sabotage increased. Talk of a general strike was spreading. Eusebio Mujal, Secretary General of the Cuban Workers' Confederation, sent word to me that he feared that he could no longer control the labor organizations.

As terroristic activities and widespread violence increased throughout the land, the government of Cuba, under the guise of maintaining law and order, stepped up its acts of retaliation.

Women and children were innocent victims of bombs set off by the terrorists in public squares, movie theaters, supermarkets, and various places where crowds might gather. The police, under their chief, Hernando Hernández, were often brutal in retaliation.

Those of the medical profession who gave aid to wounded rebels were subjected to strong-arm methods by the police. A delegate to the World Medical Association filed a protest in behalf of the Cuban medical group. As a result of this publicity, the government of Cuba did take some action to improve the situation.

Government pressure was brought to bear on judges who were considered unfriendly to the government of Cuba. Batista complained that revolutionaries were immediately released from prison by these judges on writs of habeas corpus. The press in the United States correctly published stories of cases where prisoners were immediately re-arrested, which showed disregard of the writs of habeas corpus ordered by the court.

When I spoke to the President of the unfavorable publicity and the unfriendliness such acts were causing in the United States, he replied, in effect: "When the terrorists are arrested for cowardly attacks on members of the armed services and members of the government of Cuba and innocent victims suffer, the judges release the prisoners on writs of habeas corpus before witnesses are given the opportunity to testify. We are unable to keep the culprits in jail, unless there is a suspension of constitutional guarantees."

I received word from the Prime Minister, Dr. Guell, on March 11, that he was coming over to the Embassy residence to see me on an important matter. We adjourned to the library and I could see that Dr. Guell was deeply perturbed. He told me that the situation was becoming very serious. The government was being subjected to increasing acts of terrorism and sabotage. The President had authorized Dr. Guell to tell me that he feared it would be necessary again to suspend constitutional guarantees.

President Batista knew what a bitter disappointment such news would be to me, because he and Dr. Guell knew how much effort I had made to induce Batista to restore constitutional guarantees and to lift the press censorship. So he sent his Prime Minister to prepare me for the blow before I met with him.

I told Dr. Guell that my government would adhere strictly to its policy of non-intervention, but that they would be bitterly and deeply disappointed if President Batista found it necessary again to impose the press censorship and to suspend constitutional guarantees.

Dr. Guell recalled that he had been most helpful in persuading the President to lift the suspension of guarantees. He reminded me that the President had been against such action, but had complied in order to co-operate with the United States. At this meeting Dr. Guell said that the government of Cuba would welcome the mediation of the Church and would be happy to co-operate with the Church in a peaceful solution.

The following day, March 12, 1958, the government of Cuba again suspended, for a period of forty-five days, constitutional guarantees.

On the same day I was visited at the American Embassy by my good friend, Dr. Mario Lazo, and his cousin, Dr. Marquez Sterling, political opponent of Batista and Presidential candidate of the Free Peoples Party. The purpose of the visit was to talk about the postponement of general elections. In May 1957, the Cuban government had advanced the date of the scheduled national elections to be held in 1958 from November 1 to June 1.

Dr. Marquez Sterling believed that elections should be postponed until November and that during this period of additional time every effort should be made to diminish the tension in the country, and to promote a favorable electoral climate. I learned the next day from President Batista that in accordance with the request of the opposition the elections would be postponed until November 3.

Both Dr. Marquez Sterling and Dr. Lazo believed the best way to obtain a favorable climate for general elections would be to induce Castro to call off his revolutionary activities. However, this was not possible because Fidel Castro was violently opposed to elections.

Dr. Marquez Sterling stated that Castro was opposed to elections because he believed that even if Batista were beaten in a fair election, authority would pass to the political opposition, and not to himself. He further added that Castro would make every effort to prevent elections because Castro believed that control of the government would fall in his hands in February 1959. At that time Batista would have to relinquish the reins of government to his successor and would have to step out, or openly assume the position of a dictator.

Dr. Lazo and Dr. Marquez Sterling were under the impression that there was a very good chance that fair elections could be held in the fall, if the Church, supported by the political opposition and the civic organizations, with the co-operation of the government, would make an all-out effort to create an atmosphere which was conducive to holding free and open elections. It was hoped that the United States would lend its blessing and would give its support to such a solution.

These gentlemen thought that the political opposition would win in a fair election in the fall. Even a poor opposition candidate could win over a good government candidate—assuming that the elections were to be honest.

We discussed the possibilities of my obtaining the approval of the United States to my suggesting to Batista that he leave the country; also that Batista, before departing, set up a provisional government to be supported by the United

States. It was their opinion that Batista would not turn over the government to a successor government or to a winning opposition candidate unless he had satisfactory guarantees that the army leadership would not be replaced and that no reprisals would be taken against his followers. If it were possible to obtain such guarantees, it was their opinion that Batista would not refuse to relinquish the Presidency. I questioned whether I would be able to obtain such support from the State Department.

Dr. Mario Lazo and Dr. Marquez Sterling agreed it was necessary for the government of Cuba to renew the suspension of constitutional guarantees in order to maintain itself in the face of the present revolutionary activities. It was their opinion the government would survive these activities and by concentrated efforts the government of Cuba could still knock out Castro. However, Batista could not delay much longer, as uncertainty and widespread fear were beginning to work in Castro's favor. Obviously, constitutional guarantees would have to be restored before elections.

Dr. Marquez Sterling said he had a very bad opinion of Batista. Yet, as much as he hated Batista, Castro would be ten times worse. The Cuban stateman said the only rational solution to Cuba's problem was a peaceful solution and that he would support any course that would lead to such a solution. He was willing to support a renewal of suspension of guarantees by Batista at that time, if it was accompanied by postponement of elections and by guarantees that the elections would be honest.

On March 13, the day after Dr. Guell had visited me at the Embassy, I received word from the Prime Minister that the President would receive me at Kuquine at seven o'clock. When we met in his study, surrounded by busts of Abraham Lincoln, of whom Batista was a great admirer, I could not help but notice that he showed no signs of wear and tear. One might say that ice water appeared to flow in his veins. For a man who had been going through daily crises he appeared outwardly completely calm. As usual, Dr. Guell was present. He looked tired and haggard.

Batista stated that the increase in sabotage and terrorism and general increased tension in the country had again forced him to suspend constitutional guarantees. However, he was confident that he could control the situation and was increasing the size of the army in order to give proper protection to the people of Cuba, and also to give protection to American lives and to American property.

It later developed that the expanded army was not of much use as the troops were not properly trained. The officers were more interested in corruption and enjoying the opportunities for graft. Supplies and weapons were allowed to pass through the lines to the rebels for cash.

Batista told me of his willingness to accede to all reasonable requests from the Harmony Commission and to co-operate with the Commission in order to have an atmosphere favorable to general elections. Batista believed that the National Harmony Commission had made a grave mistake. It was his understanding that the Commission would solicit the assistance of the political opposition, business, Church, civic organizations, and the press; then, after obtaining an agreement between these groups and himself, it was his understanding that the Commission would approach the revolutionaries. On the contrary, the Commission had contacted Castro before taking such steps. The result was that they were rejected by Castro and the Commission was dissolved.

Batista said the increase in armed forces would require additional arms and asked whether the government of Cuba could expect delivery of arms already negotiated for with the United States.

To my knowledge, I said, there was no change of policy

regarding the sale of arms to the Cuban government, except that the State Department wished to be advised when arms were being used for security purposes. The reason for this was that the United States wanted to enforce the provision in the Treaty which required the government of Cuba to consult with the United States when using any grant-aid equipment for purposes other than hemisphere defense.

At this meeting I spoke to the President about the alleged police brutality of Captain Sosa and advised him that the press was making much of this in the United States. He told me that he had ordered the police to make an investigation; that if the investigation substantiates the charges, he would take action. "The man is a monster," he said. Batista never did take action.

We discussed general elections and dates which would be set by the Tribunal and he stated he would make a public pledge that elections would be completely honest, and that he would accede to all reasonable requests of the opposition, such as (a) asking the world press to witness the elections, (b) asking the United Nations and the OAS to send observers. He further stated that he was prepared to grant general amnesty in the coming elections so that the Revolutionists would go to the polls. However, they would have to pledge to leave their guns behind.

Batista said that he was absolutely certain the Communists were aiding and abetting the overthrow of the Cuban government. I agreed that it was naïve for anyone to think that the Communists would not be taking advantage of political conditions in Cuba. However, I would need definite proof to convince the State Department.

I suggested for Batista's consideration that he invite the leaders of all responsible civic groups, Church, labor, press, and the political opposition to discuss the best possible means for creating an atmosphere conducive to holding free and open elections. I further suggested that he give full publicity to the provisions of the electoral laws and that he should issue a statement that the government of Cuba would abide by these laws.

Batista was receptive to the suggestion and assured me that he would comply with all reasonable requests. However, he added that he did not intend to step down from office until February 24, 1959, when his term expired. This would give the new President time to set up his administration to carry on. "It is the responsibility of the government of Cuba to preserve law and order and to prevent possible retaliation against my government between election time and February 1959," said the President.

Batista assured me that he would welcome an honorable retirement and that the best way to obtain this was through honest elections.

On March 14, 1958, the day after my meeting with President Batista at Kuquine, the State Department issued an order suspending the shipment of 1,950 Garand rifles which had been purchased by the government of Cuba and were on the docks ready for delivery by boat to Cuba.

Fidel Castro was successful in establishing espionage agents in the Cuban Embassy in Washington, D.C. These agents kept Castro in the Sierra Maestra fully informed.

Revolutionaries and sympathizers of the Cuban revolutionaries in New York had information of the rifles and their contemplated disposition. The revolutionaries even knew the serial numbers on the rifles. The Washington representatives of the revolutionaries brought a great deal of pressure to bear on the State Department to hold up this shipment. This pressure was successfully applied just at the time when President Batista announced that he would again suspend constitutional guarantees.

The Cuban desk at the State Department was sure that

leakages were coming out of the Cuban Embassy in Washington. There were only two places that one could obtain the serial numbers on these rifles—either from the War Department or the Cuban Embassy. I warned the Prime Minister and also President Batista of our belief that Castro's spies were planted in the Cuban Embassy in Washington, D.C. I even went further: I suggested to Cuban Ambassador Arroyo that it would be in the best interests of his government if he removed the entire staff, which was small, of the Cuban Embassy and installed completely new personnel, in order to be sure that he had divested the Embassy of Castro's spies. It has since been definitely established that there were Castro spies planted in the Cuban Embassy in Washington.

On the same day, March 14, 1958, I was instructed by the State Department to notify the government of Cuba that the United States was suspending shipment of all arms. Yet I was instructed to assure the government of Cuba that there was no change in the basic policy of the United States; that the steps enacted to suspend the arms shipments were taken only because of the great criticism and pressure being brought to bear by the press in the United States and by members of Congress.

Representative Charles Porter of Oregon, and Representative Adam Clayton Powell of New York, were helpful to the Castro cause. One of the arduous tasks of the State Department was to placate Congressman Porter who was carrying the torch for the revolutionaries. Regarding Congressman Powell I quote from an article in the January 5, 1959, *Washington Star*, written by Robert K. Walsh, *Star* staff writer:

Representative Powell told a news conference that he had been working hand in glove with followers of Fidel Castro in the United States since March, 1958. He said he had nothing to do with arms shipments, but sought information to acquaint Congress and the American people with the Castro movement. He (Powell) announced that he was asking President Eisenhower to move for immediate recognition of the Castro regime, and the sending of about two million dollars as a loan or grant to assist the government.

He also urged the recall of Earl E. T. Smith as United States Ambassador to Cuba. He described Mr. Smith as being 100 percent against Castro.

On the other hand, many other members of both houses of the Congress, such as Senator George Smathers, Democrat, of Florida, were aware of the Marxist leanings of Fidel Castro for many, many months before he came to power.

Before the Sub-Committee of the United States Senate on Internal Security, I testified on August 30, 1960:

Primarily I would say that when we refused to sell arms to the Cuban government and also by what I termed intervening by innuendo (which was persuading other friendly governments not to sell arms to Cuba) that these actions had a moral, psychological effect upon the Cuban armed forces which was demoralizing to the *n*th degree.

The reverse, it built up the morale of the revolutionary forces. Obviously, when we refused to sell arms to a friendly government, the existing government, the people of Cuba and the armed forces knew that the United States no longer would support Batista's government.

On March 14, the Embassy learned that the Civic Co-ordinating Committee, consisting of all civic groups of Cuba, was seriously considering making a public statement against the Cuban government.

In order not to impair the future usefulness of the Civic Co-ordinating Committee to act as a mediating body in any future peaceful solution, I felt that the Committee should know, before making a public statement, that Batista was prepared to create a favorable atmosphere in which to hold general elections and to engender a feeling of confidence in the people of Cuba that the elections would be honest. Hence, I believed it was incumbent upon me to confer with Dr. Raúl de Velasco, Chairman of the Co-ordinating Committee as well as President of the National Medical Association.

In our conference, I made it clear that the United States government had a firm position of non-intervention and was not in any way recommending that Dr. de Velasco's group use my information to talk to the government. Yet I did feel that the civic group should be aware of the fact that there might be a chance for success if it was their desire to approach Batista.

According to Dr. de Velasco, the Civic Co-ordinating Committee had more or less come to a final decision to make the statement. However, Dr. de Velasco said he would report our conversation to his Committee.

In order to avoid any future possibility of criticism, I informed Prime Minister Guell of my conversation with Dr. de Velasco. The Prime Minister said he approved and would inform the President.

Four days later, the civic groups issued a statement to the people of Cuba calling on the President to resign. It was an unsigned statement; so the document, in my opinion, did not necessarily impair the usefulness of the civic organizations in any possible future mediation which they might care to take part in.

On the night of March 15, I was informed by the former Cuban Minister of Public Works and the incumbent Cuban Ambassador to the United States, Nicolas Arroyo, at the home of the Prime Minister that the government of Cuba was greatly concerned that the United States government had found it necessary to suspend the shipment of arms to the friendly government of Cuba. He said the government of Cuba needed the arms as they were planning a big push against Castro. His words were, "The troops cannot be armed with toothpicks. They need guns."

At the same time, Dr. Guell reminded me that the government had always taken the position that it did not wish to embarrass the United States, so if the United States had any intention of canceling the arms shipments please to inform the government of Cuba. Then the Cuban government would cancel all their outstanding orders and would attempt to purchase these arms from other nations. Officially, the United States had only suspended the shipment of arms.

It was my suggestion that he put his remarks in the form of a memorandum from the government of Cuba to the United States and I would see that it was forwarded immediately to my government. I then went on to convey the assurances of the United States government that there was no change in basic attitude. Yet I knew that after March 12 this was not true.

March 12, 1958, is an important date in Cuban history. After that date it was no longer possible to engender any support in the State Department for the Batista government. It was on March 12 that Batista found it necessary to renew the suspension of constitutional guarantees and to reimpose censorship of the press. On the same day Raúl Castro successfully managed to establish a second front in the Sierra Cristal Mountains. This was a serious blow to the government of Cuba and greatly increased enthusiasm among the Fidelistas.

For months I had used every means of persuasion to convince Batista to restore constitutional guarantees in the island. Overruling the advice of his confidants he complied and did so on January 25. The Department, believing this to be a big step in the right direction, assumed a waiting attitude. As I mentioned before they agreed to renew delivery instructions on the twenty armored cars, which had been on order for some time.

Now, after approximately seven weeks, the strong man was forced to clamp down again because of the stepped-up activities of the terrorists. The waiting attitude ended. The

Rightist-dictator-haters and the pro-Castro elements, whose estimate of the situation was that Batista could only control through strong-arm methods, were back in charge.

I reminded the Department that to publicize their decision to suspend arms shipments and to enforce the amendment which required Cuba to consult with the United States before using arms for any purpose other than hemispheric defense would have a devastating psychological effect. If Batista should fall after these decisions had been publicized, the United States might well be blamed for the overthrow of the government of Cuba and for the resulting chaos and bloodshed.

Even though Batista had again suspended constitutional guarantees, it was my recommendation that we continue our policy of trying to obtain a favorable atmosphere in Cuba in which to hold general elections. If we were not prepared to salvage the situation by supporting a National Unity government (which would include the sale of arms to such government) then this was the only remaining logical course for the United States to follow.

On March 17 at a meeting of the country team (composed of chiefs of all sections of the Embassy, chiefs of all American agencies serving in Cuba, including the ranking military officers of the Mutual Defense Assistance Program), I outlined the change of policy of the United States government toward Cuba which was indicated by the suspension of the shipment of arms to them.

It was clear that there would no longer be any support to the existing government of Cuba.

On March 17 Jules Dubois, correspondent of the *Chicago Tribune*, whose anti-Batista convictions had become an obsession, came to the Chancellery of the American Embassy. When he came into my office his opening words were to the effect that the fall of Batista was inevitable and when would I get on the bandwagon to get rid of the s.o.b. He insisted that

Cuba would not have elections and said he thought the State Department should issue a statement which would bring about the overthrow of the government of Cuba.

I repeated that we were looking for a peaceful solution and stated that the fall of the government of Cuba would be followed by a blood bath. I further repeated that the State Department had no intention of making such statements and thereby openly intervening in the affairs of Cuba.

Raúl Menocal, former Mayor of Havana, and Secretary of Commerce in Batista's Cabinet, narrowly missed assassination as a man fired seven bullets at him and missed him. Two bullets broke the arm of the secretary who was with him. Menocal said he was looking straight into the man's face and could see the fire coming out of the gun, and probably five bullets were fired before he ducked. Menocal was unguarded. This was another attempt on the part of the terrorists to assassinate members of the government of Cuba.

On the evening of March 17 I was notified by Mr. Houser of the Hilton Hotel that California papers were carrying stories that all Americans should keep out of Cuba. These incidents were all part of the propaganda that was being fed to the American public to help bring about the overthrow of the government of Cuba. Mr. Houser wanted to know if there was anything drastic going on, because two days later the hotel expected 300 guests for the big gala opening of the Hilton Hotel. I told Mr. Houser that as far as the Embassy knew, the Hilton Hotel opening would take place without incident.

On March 18 I again recommended to the State Department that they fulfill their commitment and live up to their promise to deliver the twenty armored cars. According to my instructions I had informed President Batista that he could expect delivery. However, I had indications that the Department was not going to live up to its commitment.

The action on the part of the United States in suspending

the shipment of arms had a devastating psychological effect on the government of Cuba—and the reverse, it gave a great psychological uplift to the revolutionaries. This action was interpreted by the people of Cuba as a withdrawal of support for Batista, as in fact it was.

The Cuban government objected to our actions as being contrary to the 1928 Havana Convention on the Rights and Duties of States in the event of civil strife. They requested that arms shipments be renewed, as both the United States and Cuba were signatories.

On March 21 it was officially announced by the government of Cuba that elections would be postponed until November 3, 1958. This announcement was in keeping with the statement made to me by Batista.

On March 24 I sent a telegram to the State Department again requesting a continuation of shipment of arms, in view of the fact that the President had publicly declared that he would accept any reasonable demands from the opposition to hold honest elections and create the proper atmosphere for the elections; and in view of the fact that he was giving protection to and safe-guarding American lives and American property. I also based the request for renewal of shipment of arms on my estimate of the political situation in Cuba which I had sent the day before. In this estimate I once again stated that if the government of Cuba fell, the only ones to benefit would be the Communists.

To quote a personal memorandum which I made for possible future reference:

My position has not varied. I am impartial as far as the government is concerned to the political opposition; however there is no individual group ready to take over the government of Cuba. I feel it is incumbent on me to do everything possible within my limits to obtain a peaceful solution, even though I cannot obtain the support of the State Department for any such peaceful solution.

If Batista should abdicate or be overthrown, there unquestionably would be bloodshed, chaos and vandalism. This would mean the sacrifice of many lives, including many innocent victims. The madness of the crowd or mob psychology is a frightening thing.

Near the end of March I asked the State Department, before adopting a new policy of postponement of all shipment of arms, to let me explore with Batista the possibility of Batista absenting himself from Cuba during the period of elections and the President appointing a provisional government with the support of the army to supervise the elections. This should answer the objections of the opposition that no honest elections could be held under the present administration.

The State Department replied that it did not concur with my suggestion, as it would be deemed intervention.

At a dinner given by the Peruvian Ambassador and his wife, Dr. and Mrs. Brandariz, on March 25, Prime Minister Guell took me aside after dinner to say that the 26th of July Movement was aware that 1,950 small arms had been placed on a ship and then removed and that the revolutionaries would use this information to their advantage. The Prime Minister asked me to inform my government that the government of Cuba was gravely concerned regarding the policy of the United States concerning arms shipments.

I pointed out to the Prime Minister that the official attitude of the United States had not changed toward the government of Cuba but that Batista's suspension of guarantees was a great disappointment to my government. Also the timing of the suspension of guarantees had been unfortunate, because it fell immediately after Assistant Secretary of State Rubottom's testimony before a sub-committee of the United States Senate Foreign Relations Committee. It is my understanding that Rubottom testified that the government of Cuba was making an effort to establish a proper climate for elections.

The next morning I received a telephone call from the Prime Minister saying that the government of Cuba had decided to cancel the order for twenty armored cars. We had failed to live up to our promise to deliver the cars, and the government of Cuba was trying to save face. They took this step in order not to cause embarrassment to the United States and also to show the government of Cuba's desire to co-operate with the government of the United States. However, the Prime Minister stressed the view that present arms in Cuba were obsolete and deteriorating; therefore the government of Cuba was most anxious to have the United States continue the shipment of arms which had been promised because these arms were needed in order to preserve law and order.

It was again my recommendation to the Department that they continue the shipment of arms in order that the Cuban government could preserve law and order. If our aim was to have a peaceful solution and prevent a blood bath, we should continue the shipment of arms.

On two separate occasions in March, I had meetings with Herbert Matthews of the *New York Times*. At the first meeting, on the 18th, he and Mrs. Matthews lunched with my wife and me at the Embassy residence. Earlier in the day I had spoken with Dr. Guillermo Belt who told me that in a long talk with Matthews the reporter had mentioned learning from Homer Bigart of the *Times* that I had said Castro was a bandit. Even though this upset Matthews, he did not mention the remark during lunch when he did most of the talking.

In Matthews' opinion, Batista would fall; there would be a general strike and the results would be inevitable. He said the Embassy and the United States had intervened in Cuban affairs by trying to be helpful in obtaining free and open elections. I was amused at Matthews' statement because I could not help but think how much he had been intervening in the affairs of Cuba with his strong anti-Batista editorials. Mr. Matthews would not accept the fact that the Embassy had no other course to follow.

At our second meeting, on the 26th, I found Herbert Matthews perturbed and worried about the situation. He could not understand why the government of Batista did not fall. He repeated his charges of the American government's intervention. I told Matthews that we hoped for a peaceful solution and that I would continue to strive for one no matter how remote the possibility. If my government would not assist in obtaining a peaceful solution because of the fear of intervention, then the only hope was through the intervention of the Church and the force of its prestige.

Matthews did not agree. In his opinion no peaceful solution was possible because of the pent-up emotions of the Cuban people. These emotions must have an outlet. If this were the case, I pointed out, many innocent victims would suffer.

Matthews had been in contact with the 26th of July Movement in Havana and the revolutionaries in Pinar del Rio. He said the anticipated general strike would take place, but now he was not sure of the outcome. In the opinion of the journalist, Batista made a great mistake in restoring constitutional guarantees on January 25, because Matthews was convinced that Batista would not survive.

I asked Herbert Matthews if the revolutionaries had made any plans as to a provisional government or if there was a meeting of minds as to the members of the new government. The *Times* editorial writer replied that there was no agreement except that Fidel Castro wanted Urrutia to be President. He went on to say that in his opinion Urrutia would not last long in the new government. He was a good man, but unknown.

I told Matthews that the official position of the Department was one of non-intervention; i.e., the United States would take no steps to keep Batista in office and would take no steps to remove Batista from office.

At this point, the Havana Embassy decided to send a United States Army mission plane to visit the Guantánamo Naval Base, the Freeport Sulphur Nickel mine at Moa Bay, and the United States government-owned Nicaro Nickel Mine. The purpose of sending the plane was for a tranquilizing effect and to show the interest of the American Embassy in the Americans in Oriente Province (headquarters of the revolutionaries). It was also to demonstrate to the revolutionaries that the Embassy was prepared to look after American personnel.

On the night of March 29, Father John Kelly, President of Villanova University in Cuba, appeared at the residence of the American Embassy unannounced. After cordial greetings, he informed me that the Church feared civil war and was anxious to know just what the position of the United States was. I told him we were gravely concerned and fully aware of the prevailing conditions in Cuba, and added that I believed the Church at this time was our last hope of obtaining a peaceful solution.

Father Kelly told me that the Church had been unable to contact Fidel Castro and said, "Although Bishop Serantes of Oriente saved Castro's life several times, I fear Castro is not as grateful as he should be."

Father Kelly told me of reports that Fidel, while a boy attending parish school, had a motorbike accident which left him unconscious for eight days. Many people are of the opinion that Fidel is not normal, according to Father Kelly, and attribute his lack of normality to this accident.

In the belief of the ecclesiastic, the United States government should make an extensive survey into Fidel Castro's background, as the United States might well find Castro the successor to Batista.

Father Kelly, who was well known to be anti-Batista, was much concerned over the Communist affiliations of the 26th of July Movement and feared for Cuba if Castro were to take over the government.

Father Kelly said it would be better for the United States to intervene at that time because he believed that six months after Castro assumed power, the United States would have to intervene for humanitarian reasons.

I could only say the United States would adhere to its policy of non-intervention and that we would only lend moral support to any attempts to achieve a peaceful solution sponsored by the Church. Yet it was possible that the United States would make a statement endorsing such objectives.

Father Kelly was interested to learn that I had asked the State Department for permission to contact President Batista to discuss with him the advisability of his absenting himself from Cuba, setting up a provisional government of national unity and obtaining the support of the United States for such provisional government until general elections could be held.

The conversation ended with a discussion of the anticipated general strike. It was the feeling of the Embassy that if the attempt failed for lack of organization, it was possible that the revolutionaries might then be willing to conciliate. If the government of Cuba crushed the strike with great loss of life it would be difficult to predict the aftermath. If the strike was successful the government of Cuba could fall—then there would be bloodshed for an indefinite period.

The immediate reaction by Batista to our suspension of arms shipments was to cancel all other outstanding orders for arms from the United States government. He attempted to counteract the adverse publicity by making it appear that the government was well able to obtain arms from outside sources. However, President Batista informed me on numerous occasions that the suspension of arms on the part of the United States retarded his program by at least six months, because these orders had to be replaced with other governments. The government of Cuba was able to purchase war matériel from the Dominican Republic, England, Italy, and other countries. The result was a conglomeration of different types of arms from various countries.

The revolutionaries were continuing to receive shipments of arms from the United States, Venezuela, Mexico and other nations. Also the revolutionaries were able to obtain arms from the Cuban armed forces. Some members of the Cuban army were not averse to selling arms to the revolutionaries. Some arms were obtained through capture and some through desertion. Dynamite and high explosives were stolen by the rebels from the American mining camps. Rebels made land mines and hand grenades from the high explosives and dynamite stolen from American companies.

In addition to the suspension of the shipment of arms to Cuba, the State Department was bringing additional pressure to bear on the government of Cuba by calling to its attention the violation of the provisions of the Military Defense Assistance Program with Cuba which stated that the use of military equipment for any other purpose than hemispheric defense must have prior consent of the United States. The United States government maintained that certain equipment had been used by the Cuban armed forces in crushing the revolt at Cienfuegos in September 1957.

Pressure was brought to bear on the government of Cuba by stating that an infantry battalion, which had been equipped through the Military Defense Assistance Program, was being used in Oriente Province against the Castro forces. When I questioned President Batista regarding this, he said it was impossible at that stage to obtain exact information on the

deployment of this battalion, as it had been absorbed throughout the expeditionary forces and had been deployed throughout the various combat units of the army.

Upon instructions from the State Department, I informed
Prime Minister Guell that my government expected all Military Defense Assistance Program equipped and trained personnel to be recalled from fighting the revolutionaries.

The Fourth Floor of the State Department was under
constant and heavy pressure from the representatives of the
revolutionaries in Washington and from many important rebels
in exile. Some of these revolutionary leaders had at one time
been arrested by Batista, only to be released from prison later
and permitted to seek asylum in the United States.

Batista was inclined to accede to pressure and release his
enemies. At one time or another, many of the prominent revolutionists had been apprehended by Batista—including Fidel
Castro and Manuel de Varona. The release of Castro and his
supporters later helped bring about Batista's downfall. Batista
was governed by a strange, contradictory combination of im-
pulses. Although he was termed a ruthless dictator, in all the
years he was the dominant power in Cuba the death penalty
was outlawed. It was the "savior of the Cuban people," Fidel
Castro, who reinstated the death penalty and put it to shock-
ing and excessive use against the enemies of his revolution.

The representatives of the revolutionaries in Washington
were exerting constant pressure on the State Department
regarding the use of Military Defense Assistance Program
equipment in Cuba. The State Department continued to exert
pressure on the government of Cuba regarding the violations
of these provisions through the Cuban Embassy in Washington
and through the American Embassy in Havana.

Early in March 1958, a formal note was delivered to the
Cuban government bringing these matters to their attention
and requesting a report. The note was embarrassing to the

(98)

government of Cuba and they deliberately delayed answering the note from the United States government. I was instructed to remind the Prime Minister from time to time and to ask him when the State Department could expect a reply.

At a meeting with the Mission chiefs, I requested that they avoid all publicity and to be sure not to have their pictures taken in connection with arms which were in Cuba under the Military Defense Assistance Program. I emphasized the necessity that all their activities be guided with the utmost discretion, as the State Department was under great pressure from the Cuban revolutionaries regarding the activities of our missions. The State Department informed the Cuban exiles that the American missions in Cuba were serving a useful purpose and were living up to the provisions of the Treaty, under which they were established, which was to assist the government of Cuba in the training of their military forces for hemispheric defense. Also all mission personnel, including the attachés, were reminded not to be near combat areas. Otherwise the United States would be accused of actively aiding and abetting the government forces.

I was told by both President Batista and Prime Minister Guell that the Cuban government was fighting for its life against terrorists and Communist-inspired revolutionists. Batista added the government of Cuba was friendly to the United States and supported the United States wholeheartedly in its fight against Communism. He could not understand the United States intervention on behalf of Castro in his hour of need.

Batista further pointed out that the Military Defense Assistance Program agreement was made between Cuba and the United States in 1952 when the President of Cuba was Dr. Prio Socarras and prior to Batista assuming office. The United States military missions were established a year earlier when Dr. Prio was President.

I explained to the President that the reasons why our

(99)

government was forced to suspend shipment of arms was due to public pressure and pressure from members of Congress who did not understand our selling arms to the government of Cuba to be used by Cubans to kill Cubans.

In March 1958, the State Department publicized the suspension of shipment of 1,950 Garand rifles. The psychological effect of this release was damaging to the government of Cuba. Prime Minister Guell informed me that the government of Cuba was greatly concerned over the timing and necessity for this release. Prime Minister Guell did not believe it was necessary for the government of the United States to publicize this action.

President Batista informed me that he had learned from his Ambassadors to several nations that the State Department had persuaded these nations not to sell arms to the government of Cuba. This he also considered intervention in the affairs of Cuba on behalf of the terrorists. Upon inquiry at the State Department I found Batista's story to be true. Certain officers on the Fourth Floor of the State Department, when approached by representatives of other nations regarding the sale of arms to Cuba, had made it clear that the United States would look with disfavor upon such sales; although the United States was fully aware and realized that the final decision in such matters rested solely within the jurisdiction of a sovereign nation. Such intervention by innuendo was part of the campaign to bring about the downfall of the Batista government.

This pressure continued until American citizens, including American Marines and sailors, were kidnaped by Raúl Castro.

On March 18 I received a visit from Dr. Guillermo Belt with the good tidings that the Church might re-enter the picture. His information came from the Cardinal, and Dr. Belt informed me that he was using his influence along that line.

Dr. Jorge de Cubas came to the American Embassy for a visit on March 19 to find out the attitude of the United States government. Dr. de Cubas was a member of the law firm of Lazo y Cubas, probably the most outstanding and best-known law firm in Havana. Dr. de Cubas is a scholar, intelligent and well-informed. This visit was the second time that he had come to see me in a relatively short period of time.

On his previous visit a few days earlier Dr. de Cubas had called on me to inquire if there was any change in the attitude of the United States government. Dr. Jorge de Cubas had visited Eusebio Mujal, leader of the Cuban labor movement (Confederación de Trabajadores de Cuba), and informed me that Mujal was extremely concerned over the attitude of the Church and the attitude of the United States government toward the government of Cuba. If the attitude of the United States government toward Batista was changing, Mujal would not likely stand firm. At our first meeting I told Dr. de Cubas that the attitude of the United States had not changed. Cuba was a friendly government recognized by the United States and we would continue our friendly relations. There was no change in United States-Cuban relations. I further stated that the United States did not change its relations with a friendly government because conditions might become untenable for that government.

At our second meeting on March 19, Dr. de Cubas told me that had it not been for my assurances during the previous interview, Eusebio Mujal might very well have left Cuba. As I pointed out earlier, Batista remained in power because he had the support of the army, the labor leaders, and a good economy. Had Mujal left Cuba, one of the main props under Batista would have been eliminated, because Mujal controlled the Labor Movement for Batista.

I learned from Dr. de Cubas that Archbishop Perez Serantes of Oriente Province had an interview with President Batista on the previous day. Bishop Martin Villaverde of Matanzas Province had also spoken with Batista and had reassured Batista that the Church was not opposed to him. Bishop Villaverde suggested to President Batista that a provisional government be established in Cuba to supervise general elections. For this to be successful, the provisional government must have the support of the army. Batista was to withdraw; and according to the law, the Senior Justice of the Supreme Court would head the provisional government. Although Batista was noncommittal, Bishop Martin Villaverde felt sufficiently encouraged to plan an interview with Fidel Castro.

Dr. de Cubas asked me if there was any possibility of my being able to obtain the support of the United States regarding this plan. I told Dr. de Cubas that I had already discussed this with the State Department on numerous occasions. The decision of the Department was that they would not support any plan, because of the United States policy of non-intervention. They would be willing to endorse such a plan and lend their moral support only when and if it proved successful.

Dr. de Cubas said that Bishop Martin Villaverde was prepared to go ahead and carry on the negotiations as an individual. If the mission was not successful, then Bishop Martin as an individual would be able to assume the blame.

The Church obviously was prepared to inject itself again into the picture. The Church was annoyed with the position taken by the United States government. If the government of Cuba should fall during these negotiations, the Church would receive the blame. It was the feeling of the Church that the United States should also be willing to share such responsibility.

In the meantime at the Embassy we went ahead with our emergency evacuation plans in case the government of Cuba was overthrown. Consul General Brown had produced the plan. Under the supervision of Minister Counselor Braddock quantities of stickers bearing the American flag (for display on their houses) were being delivered. We obtained from the Department $25,000 in cash to keep in the Embassy safe in order to provide for the needs of Americans in the event of chaotic conditions.

On March 29, I met with Stanley Fordham, the British Ambassador, at the Havana Biltmore Club and advised him that in case of emergency it was our hope that the British government and the United States government would work as closely as Siamese twins. The American Embassy wanted the British Ambassador to know that all of our facilities would be at their service, and I brought him up to date on our plans.

I had the same conversation with the Canadian Ambassador, and also assured him that in case of emergency the facilities of the American Embassy were at his disposal.

Mrs. Daniel Braddock, wife of the Minister Counselor, Mrs. Eugene Gilmore, wife of the chief of the Economic Division, and my wife prepared and typed out a set of plans in the event of emergency evacuation to be followed by the wives of Embassy officers. The memorandum covered much of what was expected of the American women attached to the Embassy—such as filling the bathtub with water, preparing food in advance, staying indoors, etc.

The feeling of uneasiness was spreading to all groups. Many of the social leaders were losing their confidence in the survival of Batista and were considering another haven. Now that the ship seemed to be foundering many of these people, who eight months before were violently pro-Batista, were now beginning to be outspokenly against the present regime.

Serafin Romualdo, labor leader, arrived with a delegation for the opening of the Hilton Hotel. He told me he was afraid to be seen with Batista because he did not wish to be considered either pro-Batista or anti-Batista. Romualdo previously had asked me whether he should be present for the opening. I told him he had better use his own judgment. From labor leaders to social leaders—all were prepared to scuttle the ship now that they had a feeling of impending disaster.

By March 31 the Church was divided in its attitude toward obtaining a peaceful solution in Cuba. The Archbishop of Oriente Province, Perez Serantes, was not willing to ask for a truce. Nevertheless, he had made an appeal through a pastoral letter on Sunday, March 31, asking for peace. He did not ask for a truce. The majority of people in Oriente Province did not want a truce. Oriente was the headquarters of the rebels.

From April 1 to April 5 was the deadline set by the Castro people for an all-out general strike and calling on everybody to participate in the strike. Castro vowed to start his total war against Batista at this time.

In Havana, which Castro must capture to win Cuba, the situation was tense, but apparently normal as late as the first of April. By this time the city was full of American newspaper people anticipating the outbreak of the general strike and the possibility of civil war.

American newspapers were exploiting the news in favor of the revolutionaries and were exaggerating the chaotic conditions in Havana. The bearded rebels in their curious uniforms aroused interest and provided much copy, but accounts of chaotic conditions in Cuba were not accurate and added to Cuba's difficulty.

Conditions were quiet in Havana that week, yet the Castro people continued to harass American properties. One hundred and fifty armed revolutionaries walked into the American Nickel properties at Moa Bay and stopped the operations of the mining company for one day. This was not very difficult as there were only a few soldiers there at the time. One corporal was killed. This was a typical hit-and-run raid.

On March 30 a very large shipment of arms was captured by the government of Cuba and the government also obtained the names of the people to whom they were consigned.

Early in March I had information from Dr. Guillermo Belt which led me to believe that the general strike would not be a success. Dr. Belt learned from a large financial contributor to the Directório Revolucionário (DR) that the DR movement had sent word to Castro that they would appoint the Mayor, Chief of Police and the leaders of the political government in Havana upon the successful termination of the general strike.

The word came back from Fidel Castro that all appointments would be made by Fidel, himself, and that no one else had authority to make appointments. The leaders of the DR were indignant and sent back word to Fidel Castro that if this was his attitude, they would not participate in the general strike. Ever since the attack on the Presidential Palace by the DR movement in March 1957, jealousy had existed between the 26th of July Movement and the DR. This was another indication that Fidel intended to run the government all by himself and would co-operate with no other authority.

I had learned from experience that Dr. Belt's information was reliable, so I anticipated that the general strike would be unsuccessful. Although the Embassy had evidence that the Communists were actively supporting the 26th of July Movement in their plans to make the general strike effective, I still did not believe the general strike would succeed. Without the participation of the DR the strike could not be successful in the Province of Havana. Unless it was successful in the Province of Havana, it was doomed for failure. Our prognostications were later proved correct.

Just prior to April 9 the armed forces of the Republic were on the defensive. The government knew it must reinforce its position, as it would be a mistake to negotiate with the rebels from a weak position.

Amongst the opposition there was a complete division as

to what they would negotiate for, except for the postponement of the election date. The government of Cuba at the request of the political opposition had moved forward the election date, so that the proper changes could be made in the electoral code. The government of Cuba would welcome a truce only after its position was reinforced, as it believed that the rebels would not honor a truce but would continue violence and sabotage, and then accuse the government of violating the truce.

The attitude as to the acceptability of a truce depended on which side was in the ascendancy. At this particular time, before the elections and before the general strike, the rebels believed their position to be at a high point and they were optimistic about their chances of taking over the government of Cuba. Therefore they were not in the frame of mind to discuss a truce.

The situation in Cuba was like dropping soda into a glass of water. It fizzles for a while and then stops. When it was fizzling, the rebels appeared to be in the ascendancy. When it stopped, the government of Cuba appeared to be restoring its dominant status.

Dr. Guell, who also held the office of Prime Minister, was a mild, gentlemanly diplomat. He professed himself to be against violence and against dictatorships, but confessed that sometimes the police in their resort to violence were too zealous. It was unfortunate for Foreign Minister Guell that he accepted Batista's appointment as Prime Minister. This appointment removed him from the diplomatic world and placed him side by side with Batista in his fight for political survival. Guell was sincere in his belief that under Castro there would be a Leftist dictatorship in Cuba. As regards Communism, the words of the Prime Minister were: "If Castro comes to power, the situation in Cuba will be even worse than in Guatemala. Communism will prevail."

(106)

Dr. Guell appeared sincere in his assurances that Batista wished to relinquish power to a new President, whether a government candidate or of the opposition party, who must be elected by the people and prepared to guarantee the normal democratic development of Cuba.

In response to my suggestion that the President should publicly announce this intention, Dr. Guell said he believed Batista would comply.

It was agreed between us this could be accomplished by having the President publicly support a statement along these lines to be made by the four government coalition parties. Prime Minister Guell telephoned later to say the President had agreed to making such a statement. Batista, a few days later, followed through, but the statement was not forceful enough to carry conviction.

I was authorized by the State Department to suggest to the President that he invite, in addition to the Church, opposition political leaders, labor, and civic leaders to discuss steps to insure free and open elections. I was further authorized to suggest to the President that he discuss with these leaders ways and means to obtain the co-operation of these various organizations to insure honest elections.

There can be no doubt that the decision by the State Department to suspend the shipment of arms to Cuba was the most effective step taken by the Department of State in bringing about the downfall of Batista. There was hardly ever a day that went by that this subject was not brought to my attention by the government of Cuba.

Dr. Guell graciously intimated he understood the embarrassing position in which the press and Congressional criticism in the United States had placed the Department of State. I told him Assistant Secretary Rubottom expected soon to be summoned before the Senate Foreign Relations Committee to explain the State Department's arms policy to Congress. I tried to make it clear that our friendly relationship toward the government of Cuba was unchanged.

In reporting these conversations to the State Department, I commented that I thought the majority of Cubans wanted a peaceful solution and this was also the hope and objective of the Embassy. I also reminded the State Department that it is very hard to get rid of dictatorships, although relatively easy to change dictators; that the people of Cuba were "riding the tiger" and it would be no solution merely to change tigers.

In order to save face, the government of Cuba cancelled all orders for tanks, grenades, and rifles. However, they were anxious to know if we would continue shipment of spare parts.

On April 3, I strongly recommended to the Department that favorable action be taken regarding the shipment of spare parts on order. I pointed out that the political situation in Cuba had evolved into civil war between two dominant figures, would-be dictator Castro and dictator Batista. I reminded the Department that we were consistently asking the government of Cuba to protect American property from the sabotage efforts of the revolutionaries and listed a number of United States plants which had already been damaged. I further stated that the Communists were actively supporting and co-operating with the Castro Revolutionary Movement in their efforts to make the anticipated general strike effective.

Chapter XIII

Guantánamo Naval Base

OUTSIDE THE CONTINENTAL LIMITS of the United States, one of the major American Naval Bases is at Guantánamo Bay in the province of Oriente.

When I was Ambassador to Cuba, there were approximately 2,500 Marines and sailors situated at the base and there were approximately an additional 2,500 relatives of the servicemen. Also the base employed in the neighborhood of 5,000 Cubans.

The water supply at Guantánamo comes from a plant at Yateras located in Cuban territory, five miles from the base. This plant was owned by a Cuban company and operated by

Cubans. The water came to the base through a pipe line. The plant was guarded by Cuban soldiers.

In March 1958, I learned from the American Base Commander, Admiral R. B. Ellis, that he was very much concerned regarding the safety of the Yateras plant and requested that the government of Cuba be so advised, as there were rumors that the revolutionaries would shut off the water supply by damaging the plant. There was also the problem that only the local Cuban personnel were familiar with the operations of the plant.

I asked President Batista for permission for the American Base commander to send non-uniformed Base personnel to Yateras in order that they might familiarize themselves with the operations of the plant.

Batista wanted joint protection of the plant between the United States Navy and the Cuban Army which we could not grant. The State Department wished it to be made clear that the United States would not in any way impose upon the sovereignty of Cuba and that under no circumstances could American troops be used alongside Cuban troops in protecting the water plant. I informed the President that the armed forces of the United States would be utilized in the operation of the plant only in the event that the government of Cuba was unable to provide the necessary protection. In the event that the government of Cuba found it necessary to withdraw the troops from the plant, I asked the President for permission to use American Marines.

It was clearly understood that no Cuban personnel would remain on the site of the plant, when, as, and if American personnel were dispatched by the Guantánamo Base Commander.

On April 4 and 5, extensive negotiations were carried on between Prime Minister Guell and myself. We finally came up with an agreement which would permit the Americans to learn how to operate the aqueduct. The Cubans would have the main responsibility for protecting the water supply. If it was necessary to withdraw the Cuban troops for an emergency, United States Marines would have advance permission to take over the protection of the plant.

I took particular pains to make sure that the government of Cuba understood that American Marines could not, and would not, fight alongside Cuban troops. This was to be an informal arrangement, which would terminate when the present emergency ended. A few days later the American Base Commander was granted permission by Batista for the use of Marines under the conditions outlined, if it was deemed necessary.

The State Department authorized the Base Commander to assume full responsibility for the protection of the water supply at Guantánamo, if the government of Cuba was unable to give proper protection. With the approval of the government of Cuba, the United States Navy arranged for the training of non-uniformed personnel in the operation of the plant.

In April, Batista told me the troops were doing well in Oriente Province, where the water plant was situated, and that the government of Cuba had things well in hand.

By July he said, "The soldiers at the plant are like sitting ducks. The rebels can ambush these troops any time they so desire."

In late July the Cuban troops guarding the plant were withdrawn. The Naval Base Commander requested authority to dispatch Marines to the plant. I received permission from the State Department to grant such authority to the American Naval Base Commander, in accordance with our agreement of the previous April. On July 28 a detachment of United States Marines took over the water plant at Yateras.

The United States had no other choice. It was absolutely necessary to protect the water supply, because 10,000 people had no other source of water. Also, the action taken in dispatching the Marines for the protection of the plant was done with the advance approval of the government of Cuba.

It was my belief that Fidel Castro would resent the dispatching of American Marines to the plant because it made it possible for the government of Cuba to withdraw troops from guard duty for active use in the combat area. Thereupon, Fidel Castro screamed, "Intervention!" and demanded the immediate recall of the American troops, asserting that the United States was infringing upon the sovereignty of Cuba. The Communists renewed their old charges of Yankee imperialism.

The State Department succumbed to the pressure of the representatives of the revolutionaries in Washington, D.C., and requested the Navy Department to withdraw the Marines from the plant. A press release was planned by the State Department announcing the withdrawal of the Marines.

Late the night of July 30 Prime Minister Guell came to the residence of the American Embassy to protest the alleged press release regarding withdrawal of the Marines, about which he learned through the Cuban Embassy in Washington. The release was to be issued by the State Department without informing the government of Cuba. As a result of a telephone call to Assistant Secretary Rubottom I was able to hold up the Department's release until the government of Cuba was informed of the wording. This gave the government of Cuba an opportunity to make a simultaneous release of their own to save face.

On July 31 our Marines were withdrawn and the water plant was left temporarily unguarded. On August 2 the government reassigned Cuban troops to guard the plant, and indicated that American Marines had been used at the plant only during a replacement interval of Cuban soldiers. After the withdrawal of the Marines, the State Department conferred directly with representatives of Castro in Washington, asking them to desist from tampering with the water supply of the base and pointed out there could be unfavorable reaction in the United States.

The fear that the rebels might shut off the water supply continued throughout the year 1958.

President Batista assured me from time to time that he would give proper protection to the plant. In spite of his assurances, he was unable to do so as this territory came under rebel control.

In November the rebels again started harassing activities against the Yateras plant. In accordance with well-known Communist guerrilla tactics, they shut off the water supply for one hour one day, two hours the second day, and three hours the third day. I received a request for authority to dispatch Marines to Yateras from the American Naval Base Commander. I immediately forwarded this request to the State Department, endorsing the recommendations and advising the Department that Batista had approved our request to dispatch Marines to the plant until such time as he could supply Cuban troops. I requested authority from the State Department to approve the Naval Base Commander's request if there was any further shut-off of the water supply.

The State Department, through its contacts with the revolutionaries in Washington, again appealed to Castro not to resume these unfriendly and irresponsible acts. The State Department was still trying to encourage a sense of responsibility amongst the revolutionary leaders.

President Batista said he had three choices. He asked which one of the three courses we recommended:

(A) To leave the plant unguarded.
(B) To have the plant guarded jointly by American Marines and Cuban troops.
(C) To assign approximately fifty soldiers to be sacrificed.

My word back from the State Department was to inform Batista to follow course (C). President Batista informed me that he would send Naval troops to the plant and requested permission to land Cuban Marines at the Naval Base for dispatch to the water plant. This request we could not grant, as the United States would be placed in the compromising position of actively aiding the troops of the government of Cuba.

Fortunately the Castro forces did not again shut off the water, so it was not necessary to take further action. Such irresponsible acts on the part of the revolutionaries to harass the United States were Communist-inspired and were typical of the machinations of Raúl Castro.

The use of American Marines for guard duty in Cuban territory posed a ticklish point for the State Department, even though our Marines were invited by the government of Cuba to protect the water supply which was essential for the survival of 10,000 human beings.

It was amusing for the revolutionaries to taunt, tantalize, and harass the United States because they seemed to feel we would do nothing to impair the revolution.

Chapter XIV

American Intervention and the Fall of Batista

THE DAY-BY-DAY ACTIONS of those on the Fourth Floor of the State Department shaped United States-Latin American foreign policy as far as Cuba was concerned. Stress was laid by these officers on pleasing liberal Latin American opinion, sometimes at the risk of sacrificing American self-respect.

I will list some of the day-by-day actions of those on the Fourth Floor of the State Department who shaped American foreign policy toward Cuba (not listed in order of importance):

1. Suspending the sale of arms and ammunition to the government of Cuba, which had a devastating psychological effect upon those supporting the government of Cuba. In the reverse, the action gave a great psychological uplift to the Castro followers. It forced Batista to turn to other sources for arms, entailing much delay. Also, the United States' refusal made it difficult for Cuba to obtain arms from other nations.

2. Refusal to honor outstanding and prepaid orders for arms.

3. Suspending shipment of all replacement parts for combat equipment.

4. Advising the Department of Defense not to ship controversial military equipment. Such steps were considered a withdrawal of support for the government of Cuba.

5. Not fulfilling our commitment to deliver the twenty armored cars.

6. Not living up to our promise to deliver fifteen training planes.

7. Issuing public statements that hurt the government of Cuba, aided the rebels, and did not help the United States—such as publicizing the news of suspended shipment of the 1,950 Garand rifles; publicizing the news of suspended shipment of Military Defense Assistance Program equipment; publicizing the news that the United States was shipping arms to neither the government of Cuba nor to the rebels. By such actions, the lower echelon of the State Department created the impression in the minds of the public that the United States gave the status of belligerency to the revolutionaries.

8. Intervention by innuendo—persuading other governments not to sell arms to the government of Cuba.

9. Refusing to permit military service officers, attached to the Military Assistance Advisory Groups, to carry out fully their functions as prescribed under the Hemispheric Military Assistance Program; that is, playing down all activities which could be deemed offensive to the revolutionaries.

10. Bringing pressure to bear on the government of Cuba by consistently calling to its attention the violation of the provisions of the Military Defense Assistance Program with Cuba, which stated

that the use of military equipment for any other purpose than hemispheric defense must have prior consent of the United States.

11. Bringing pressure to bear on the government of Cuba by stating repeatedly that the infantry battalion, which had been equipped through the Military Defense Assistance Program, was actively engaged in suppressing the rebellion in Oriente Province and then attempting to force the government to break up and retire from active service this infantry battalion.

12. Requesting the government of Cuba to disengage *all* the Military Defense Assistance Program equipped and trained personnel from the combat area.

13. Embarrassing the government of Cuba by delivering a formal note in March 1958 bringing these matters to their attention and requesting a report.

14. Not bringing sufficient pressure to bear on the Justice Department to enforce our neutrality laws.

15. Permitting Dr. Carlos Prio Socarras and his supporters to violate United States neutrality laws. Dr. Prio was permitted to enter the United States in the spring of 1956 on parole status. If he violated American laws, it was agreed, his parole status was automatically broken. Under the agreement, he could have been removed from the United States. Batista was convinced that Dr. Prio and his agents were the main source of supply of arms, ammunition, and bodies to the Sierra Maestra. Indictment of Dr. Prio was not obtained until the middle of February 1958. Then, he was immediately released on bail. The activities of Dr. Prio were of the greatest concern to President Batista. The President told me on numerous occasions that if the United States would control the activities of Dr. Prio, he would be able to cope with Fidel Castro.

16. Asking the Immigration Department to be lenient on certain Cuban revolutionary exiles and by permitting them to prolong their visits in this country.

17. Maintaining friendly contacts with representatives of the revolutionaries, thereby giving sympathetic audience and comfort to those who were openly advocating the overthrow of the government of Cuba.

18. Permitting Castro sympathizers and supporters in the United States to form groups and organizations engaged in fund raising and overt propaganda activities.

19. Embarrassing the government of Cuba by instructing me to obtain assurances that the government of Cuba would not bomb Cuban cities where rebels were situated, with American Military Assistance Program bombers using napalm bombs.

20. Maintaining close contact with Herbert Matthews, of the *New York Times*, who gave the impression by his editorial conduct of advocating Batista's downfall.

The following colloquy took place on September 8, 1960, when William D. Pawley, former United States Ambassador to Peru and to Brazil, testified before a sub-committee of the United States Senate to investigate the "Communist Threat to the United States Through the Caribbean":

Mr. J. G. Sourwine (chief Counsel): Mr. Ambassador, you have made clear to us in your testimony your belief that many policies with respect to Latin America have been made in the State Department not at the top level but at a lower level. As you explained it, they are made on the fourth floor and not on the fifth floor.

Is there any question in your mind that this situation affects the internal security of the United States?

Mr. Pawley: Yes, I think it has a direct bearing on this nation's security.

On June 12, 1961, Robert C. Hill, former United States Ambassador to Mexico, to Costa Rica and to El Salvador, also former Assistant Secretary of State in charge of Congressional Relations, testified as follows before the sub-committee of the United States Senate to investigate the "Communist Threat to the United States Through the Caribbean":

The Chairman (Senator Eastland): Now you state all the intelligence from the CIA and other agencies in 1957 and 1958 before

Castro grabbed power in Cuba indicated that he was pro-Communist?

Mr. Hill: I don't say all the intelligence did, Senator Eastland, but, as I said earlier, Castro and his affiliations were brought to my attention by intelligence representatives of the United States that were assigned to Mexico. They started talking to me about Castro and the problem early in 1957. I was very busy getting started in Mexico as the Ambassador and much of 1957 went by before I could review the developments in Cuba regarding Mr. Castro. The intelligence reports from our Embassy in 1958 started to pick up—and 1959—showing more and more indications of Communism, pro-Communism—and Communists that were surrounding Fidel Castro in Cuba.

The Chairman: That is correct. It picked up before he assumed power in 1959, the reports that he was pro-Communist and surrounded by Communists.

Now the question I am going to ask you is this: wasn't it your judgment that the Caribbean desk of the State Department of the United States was pro-Castro?

Mr. Hill: Before I went to Mexico?

The Chairman: Sir?

Mr. Hill: I recall the fact that in the spring of 1957 Earl Smith, who went to Cuba as the Ambassador, came to my office and asked me to talk with him about his preparations for his Cuban assignment.

I had known Ambassador Smith at the Republican conventions held in Chicago and San Francisco. I actually worked with him in 1956 in San Francisco on foreign policy matters.

I said, "Earl, I am sorry that you are going to Cuba. You might be interested to know that 'Chip' Bohlen was supposed to go to Cuba." This sort of set him back. He said, "What do you mean, that Ambassador Bohlen was going to be transferred from Moscow to Havana?" I said, "That was the plan a few months ago. Then the President and Secretary Dulles decided to send him to Manila. You are assigned to Cuba to preside over the downfall of Batista. The decision has been made that Batista has to go. You must be very careful."

The Chairman: The decision was made where?

Mr. Hill: I am talking about the corridors of the State Department, Senator.

The Chairman: But it was your judgment that the decision had been made by the State Department that Batista had to go?

Mr. Hill: I am not saying the decision at the top, but the decision down at the lower level.

The Chairman: I asked you about the Caribbean Section.

Mr. Hill: It was common knowledge in the Department of State that Batista had to go. I told Ambassador Smith this.

The Chairman: That Castro would come into power?

Mr. Hill: That is correct. I told Ambassador Smith that he should request from the Secretary of State to take men that he had confidence in, to Havana with him, including his Minister because if he was not careful, his reputation would be destroyed. I recall that we had lunch at the Chevy Chase Club along with my wife. At that time he asked me if I had any suggestions as to who might be available for the Minister's job at the Embassy in Havana. I gave him the names of Foreign Service officers that I felt could be helpful and had a knowledge of the area. None of them would accept the job. Some of the men told me privately, "I don't want to go to Havana because Castro is coming into power." They told me that there is going to be grave trouble down there. They said they had young children and did not want to become involved.

I further told Ambassador Smith not to leave the Embassy. I said, "You stay in the vicinity of your residence in the chancery until you know what is going on in Havana. Don't travel outside the area of the capital." I tried to be as helpful to him as possible.

My predecessor as United States Ambassador to Cuba, Arthur Gardner, testified on August 27, 1960, before the same sub-committee of the United States Senate that "for two years the United States was gradually making Batista feel we were pulling the rug out from under him," and that he (Gardner) had been ignored, overlooked and circumvented by the State Department.

On July 17, 1959, Spruille Braden (former Ambassador to

(120)

Colombia, Cuba, Argentina and Assistant Secretary of State for American Republic Affairs) also testified: "In early or mid-1957, I gave an interview to *Human Events,* in which I told of certain activities of Fidel Castro—now Prime Minister of Cuba —activities in respect of the Communist-inspired insurrections in Bogotá during the Inter-American Conference held in that city in April 1948, and I declared that he was either a Communist or their tool, and that his victory would bring political and economic chaos and the tyranny of Communism to Cuba.

(The interview as printed in *Human Events* of August 17, 1957, reads as follows:)[1]

Cuban Revolt

Many on the Hill are beginning to say now: "We ought to be worrying more about the Communist menace in Latin America, on our very doorstep, than about Communism in the faraway Middle East." What's really behind the revolt led by Fidel Castro against the Cuban Government, billed by the *New York Times* and the liberal press as a simple rebellion against dictatorship, comes into clearer focus from the following statement, obtained exclusively by the staff of *Human Events* from former United States Ambassador to Cuba, Spruille Braden. This retired American diplomat has long qualified as an expert not only on Cuba but also on all Latin America; having served in other posts south of the border, he has in recent years won recognition as a critical observer of the workings of the Communist apparatus in the Caribbean and South America.

Mr. Braden says of Fidel Castro, leader of the fledgling Cuban revolt, that, according to official documents he has seen, "He is a fellow traveler, if not a member of the Communist Party and has been so for a long time. He was a ringleader in the bloody uprising in Bogotá, Colombia, in April 1948, which occurred (and obviously was planned by the Kremlin) just at the time when the Pan American Conference was being held in that capital, with no less a

---

[1] I was not aware of this interview at the time. Yet it is interesting to note that it was printed only one month after I assumed my post as Chief of Mission in Havana.

person than Secretary of State George C. Marshall present. The uprising was engineered and staged by Communists, and the Colombia Government and Colombia press subsequently published documentary evidence of Fidel Castro's role as a leader in the rioting which virtually gutted the Colombian capital. The appearance of this Cuban at the head of the recent uprising in his own country stamps the insurrection as another part of the developing Communist pattern of such subversion throughout Latin America—although a number of thoroughly decent and patriotic Cubans have been misled into sympathizing with, and in some cases supporting, the Fidel Castro movement."

I also testified under oath before the same sub-committee that: "I believe that the policies are determined in the lower echelon, and by the time the higher echelon receives them, policies have already been made, and they have to live by them."

In addition to the harassing activities against American citizens, American property owners, and the Yateras water plant, American firms suffered huge losses due to sabotage, plundering, and confiscation. American Marines, sailors, and citizens were kidnaped. Cuban commercial aircraft with Americans aboard were hijacked. There were depredations against the United States government-owned $100,000,000 Nicaro Nickel properties. The revolutionaries had utter disregard for American lives and property.

Nevertheless, the liberal press and the Fourth Floor of the State Department continued to sympathize with the revolutionaries.

The Embassy in Havana maintained normal relations with the recognized, friendly government of Cuba. The Fourth Floor maintained relations with the representatives of the revolutionaries and gave sympathetic attention to their requests. Not only were rebel spokesmen cordially received, at times the Latin American corridors were filled with partisans of the Cuban revolution.

During all this period the United States gave asylum to all Cuban exiles. Many Cuban exiles were openly violating the neutrality laws and the criminal code of the United States through exportation of arms, ammunition, and bodies to the revolutionaries; by the launching of armed expeditions from Florida shores; and by giving training in demolition and sabotage to Castro volunteers. The worst offender was Dr. Carlos Prio Socarras and his agents.

The revolutionaries openly boasted that only about 10 percent of arms exported from the United States to Cuba was apprehended by the United States authorities. Arms and bodies were smuggled out of the United States by aircraft and boats to Fidel Castro in the Sierra Maestra and to Raúl Castro in the Sierra Cristal.

The harassing activities on the part of the revolutionaries against American property and against American citizens took place not only in Cuba but also in Miami. On April 4 President Batista complained that a large group of members of the 26th of July Movement were molesting Cuban pilots of Cubana Airways at the Miami Airport. Three Cuban pilots had received physical harm. The objective of the revolutionaries in Miami was to stop commercial planes from flying between Miami and Havana in accordance with their schedules.

I informed Assistant Secretary Rubottom of the President's complaint. He immediately contacted the Justice Department and also notified the two Florida Senators, Smathers and Holland. As a result, Cubana Airways was able to resume their scheduled flights.

The State Department notified the Embassy that shipments of non-combat equipment to the government of Cuba had been approved. However, it would not approve the shipment of replacement parts for combat equipment. The State Department, therefore, had decided not only to suspend the shipment of arms to Cuba, but also to suspend the shipment of all replacement parts for combat equipment.

In early April many members of the American press descended upon the city of Santiago—the headquarters of the revolutionaries—in anticipation of the general strike, and sensing that Santiago would be a better source of news than Havana.

On April 8 seven Americans were arrested in Santiago. They were representatives of the American press and American broadcasting stations. The reason given by Prime Minister Guell for their arrest was that the government of Cuba was worried about their safety. The position of the government was that if one was killed by the revolutionaries, it would be blamed on the government and it would be most embarrassing. The government was trying to discourage members of the press from going into rebel territory. Due to the efforts of Minister Counselor Braddock, First Secretary Topping, and myself we were able to obtain the release by two o'clock in the morning of all these gentlemen.

There were no Embassies of Communist countries in Cuba during Batista's Presidency. He forced the Soviet Embassy to close and took steps which brought about Russia's severance of diplomatic relations with Cuba. These steps occurred before I was appointed United States Ambassador to Cuba.

Under Batista the Bureau for Repression of Communist Activities, known as BRAC, was set up. This agency, with American aid, was in operation for years. At times, it was effective. At other times, I found it necessary to appeal for more vigorous action.

Although we had much and consistent intangible evidence of the Communist infiltration and control of the 26th of July Movement, the Communists were too smart to give us any one piece of all-conclusive and irrefutable evidence of their control of the Castro movement. Many times, I had asked President Batista and Prime Minister Guell to give me their proof with which I could further substantiate my charges to the Department that the Castro revolution was not only infiltrated, but also under the control of the Communists.

In early April, I received word from Dr. Guell that he had additional evidence to substantiate the connection between the Communists and the Castro movement. The Bureau for the Repression of Communist Activities, in connection with the police, had raided the headquarters of the Communist newspaper, *Hoy*, and had found, according to Dr. Guell, propaganda literature of the 26th of July Movement which had been printed on the same press used by the newspaper *Hoy*.

I instructed the Embassy press officer, Mr. John Williams, to investigate and report to me on the charges. From the evidence that existed, it appeared that the 26th of July propaganda literature had been turned out by the press of the Communist paper, *Hoy*.

Mr. Bruce Henderson of *Time-Life* was quite indignant that I should have sent the Embassy public relations officer to attend a press conference held by the Cuban police in which the government of Cuba presented alleged proof tying up Fidel Castro with the Communists. It was his opinion, shared by some other members of the American press, that the Cuban police had just put on a show to pin the Communist label on Castro.

Mr. Henderson was considered one of the top Latin American reporters for Time, Inc. It happened that, late that day, my wife, Florence, met him at a reception. She found Mr. Henderson to be charming and invited him to the residence for a swim and lunch—not knowing of our contretemps. We talked for hours on the Cuban situation. Although Mr.

Henderson had preconceived ideas, approaching antagonism to me, he did understand my position. I promised to keep him as fully informed as permitted on political developments; we parted, I believe, sharing a feeling of mutual respect.

On the night of April 8 I received a visit at the Embassy residence from the Papal Nuncio, Monsignor Luigi Centoz and the Bishop of Havana, Monsignor Alfredo Muller. Bishop Muller was on his way to Oriente to pick up Archbishop Perez Serantes to go up in the hills by helicopter to visit Castro to obtain a truce.

The Papal Nuncio said that because of my great interest in obtaining a truce would I assist them in mediating. I was only authorized to reaffirm the position of non-intervention of the United States and so I told them I had no authority to mediate or to take part in the preliminary demarche. If the Church were able to establish a truce, I was sure that the United States State Department would make some sort of statement showing its desire for a peaceful solution of the troublesome days in Cuba. More than that I was not authorized to promise.

The Papal Nuncio asked if the Navy would supply a helicopter to transport Archbishop Serantes and Monsignor Muller to the hills. Such a flight, I said, would create a lot of publicity and advised the Papal Nuncio against the action at that time. Then I suggested that the timing might be more propitious if they were to postpone their visit to Castro until a later date.

The proposed visit by the Church dignitaries had been cleared with President Batista ten days before when his position was a little precarious. In the next ten days Batista's position was much stronger. Therefore, I suggested that it might be prudent to clear again the visit with the President. I also had information that the general strike would take place momentarily. Any overtures for a truce would be more effective at a later date. A visit in the hills in a helicopter would attract quite a good deal of attention. It would be propitious for the Church to make sure that their expedition be successful; if unsuccessful, such a visit could place the Church in an embarrassing light.

The next morning I was thankful for the advice I had given the Papal Nuncio, because the much anticipated general strike was called on the morning of April 9.

By eleven o'clock conditions were still normal in Havana. News from the outlying provinces was different. In Oriente where the strike did not start until the afternoon, it was more or less effective. However, the real test would come in Havana. If the strike was not effective in this great city it would be broken in the rest of the island.

The strike in Havana was not effective because the student group's committee had decided not to co-operate with the 26th of July Movement. If Castro had been willing to let the Directório Revolucionário name the Mayor and other officials in the city, they would have actively co-operated and the results might have been different. Also there was no confidence on the part of the general public in Castro, and Batista had the support of the Army, police force, and labor leaders.

At 11:00 A.M. I received a telephone call from Mr. William Wieland, Director, MID, Department of State. The conversation began as follows:

Wieland: "How are things down there this morning?"

Ambassador: "Nice and quiet—the war is still being fought in the United States."

I knew the Director of MID and others in his section were hopefully expecting the general strike to be a success, and it pleased me to be able to report otherwise.

The general strike in Havana was completely ineffective and only lasted for a short while, much to the disappointment of many influential persons in the United States. There was some disruption, but Havana was back to normal in a few hours.

The rebels had boasted that 50,000 Cubans would go on strike in Havana and they were sickened by their complete failure.

At this moment, after the failure of the general strike, Batista apparently felt that he was in the ascendancy. He decided to step up the military campaign. The Fourth Floor, however, held that a resumption of strong-arm methods would not create a climate for peace. The Fourth Floor further maintained that strong-arm methods only meant fighting terror with terror, which would further turn public opinion against Batista. For Batista to seek a purely military solution was unfortunate.

The State Department instructed me to express to Batista and government officials our hope that conditions for acceptable elections would be instituted, such as: restoration of constitutional guarantees and lifting of the press censorship; invitations to OAS, the world press and UN observers to witness the elections. Batista promised to comply with every one of these suggestions and gave me his word that the elections would be honest.

Meanwhile, Fidel Castro's Miami press agents continued their thorn-in-the-side activities which harassed the Cuban government more than Castro's actual guerrilla activities. On the morning of April 10, the *Miami Herald* carried the following front-page story:

A United States Embassy spokesman in Havana told the *Herald* by telephone even before Batista's victory claim that the "incident" lasted only a short while and that Havana was back to normal within a couple of hours.

In Washington, the State Department said, however, it was prepared to evacuate United States citizens from Cuba if the fighting intensifies. They said military air transport planes and naval vessels were standing by to remove an estimated 10,000 United States citizens in the event that all-out fighting develops.

Officials said the evacuation scheme was set up in several stages. It would begin with an island-wide alarm to all United States residents to gather at pre-arranged spots to await air or sea transportation.

The Department of State immediately denied the story that the United States Navy vessels were standing by to evacuate 10,000 Americans and made the following release:

Within the past few days certain United States newspapers have published stories to the effect that the Department of State was prepared to evacuate an estimated 10,000 United States citizens from Cuba. Newspapers said military air transport planes and naval vessels were standing by to remove an estimated 10,000 United States citizens in the event all-out fighting developed. The State Department issued a statement yesterday afternoon which read as follows: "There is nothing to the story. There are, of course, United States Naval units in the vicinity and at our base in Guantánamo and at nearby installations in continental United States. These units could, of course, participate in carrying out standing plans for evacuation if this should prove to be necessary. This is normally left to the people on the scene and the Department of State has received no indication from the Embassy in Havana that they felt this to be necessary."

Minister Counselor Braddock had set up in the Embassy routine plans for evacuation of Americans if this should prove to be necessary. On the contrary, conditions were not disturbed.

The United States press continued to intervene in the affairs of Cuba by grossly exaggerating and slanting the news on violent conditions; thereby influencing public opinion in the United States and keeping American tourists away from Cuba.

Faustino Perez, right-hand man in Havana of Fidel Castro,

was in charge of the 26th of July Movement in Havana on April 9. Revolutionary leaders attempted to blame the failure of the strike on Faustino Perez. It was reported to the Embassy that Perez and other representatives of the Castro forces in Havana were planning to attack the property of United States citizens in Cuba because of their chagrin over the collapse of the strike.

The general strike was a complete failure because economic conditions were good; there was no co-ordination on the part of the revolutionaries in Havana; there was no confidence on the part of the general public in Castro outside of Oriente Province; the government of Cuba retained the full support of the armed services, the police force and the labor leaders.

The collapse of the much touted strike was a severe psychological blow to the Castro forces. Had the Department been willing this would have been an opportune time for the United States to apply pressure on Batista to make overtures for peace, to include his complete retirement from the political picture. The Cuban Episcopacy was prepared to approach Batista with concrete suggestions and sought the support of the United States. The State Department would back no solution. Yet the Department well realized that, because of our dominant position in Cuba, no solution could be successful unless fully supported by the United States.

Rebel spokesmen in Washington were pressuring the State Department to try to obtain spiritual aid to embarrass the Batista government. These partisans of the rebel cause were attempting to convince the State Department that the government of Cuba was bombing Cuban cities, where rebels were situated, with American Military Assistance Program bombers.

The State Department was told by the representatives of the revolutionaries that the rebels would try to capture some cities and the government of Cuba would use MAP-supplied bombers to drop napalm bombs obtained from the Dominican Republic. I was instructed to obtain assurances from the proper authorities that the government of Cuba would not take any of these actions.

With the advance knowledge and consent of Foreign Minister Guell, my secretary recorded his remarks made over the telephone:

> We never bomb any city or any large town. There is not the remotest possibility of any such occurrence. My government is extremely sorry to receive this kind of inquiry because it does not adjust to the real facts. There is no chance of the revolutionaries capturing any of these cities. What they do sometimes is to make a hit and run raid on a small place. We never bomb any city. I repeat, there is not the remotest possibility that we would do anything like that. We haven't even done this in the Sierra because of the farms surrounding the place. Even in combat we manage as much as possible so as not to cause many deaths. We try to capture prisoners, while the rebels shoot our soldiers when they engage in action. We have purchased arms some place else and we have paid for these arms.

At this time the Department issued a public statement saying that it was shipping arms to neither the rebels nor to the government of Cuba; by this statement the State Department created the impression that the United States considered the rebels as being on the same plane as the government of Cuba.

I pointed out in a cable to the State Department that we had given indirect aid to the rebels by not fulfilling our commitment to deliver the twenty armored cars and by publicizing the suspension of arms. I strongly recommended that we cease issuing public statements that would hurt the government of Cuba, aid the rebels, and not help the alleged impartial position of the United States.

On April 12 I wrote a memorandum for my personal

records in longhand to the effect that we were receiving more and more reports indicating that the Communist Party of Cuba (Partido Socialista Popular) was supporting the 26th of July Movement. The latest reports were from J. Edgar Hoover.

The prestige of the Castro forces had shrunk because of the failure of the general strike. As a result, the revolutionaries believed some drama was necessary to regain the spotlight.

On April 15 the Embassy learned from a reliable source in the International Co-operation Administration (Point Four Program) that the Castro forces were going to kidnap the American Ambassador. Because of loss of prestige, as the result of the failure of the general strike, the 26th of July Movement wished to regain the limelight through some publicity stunt. It later developed that they dropped the idea to kidnap me. Instead the forces of Raúl Castro planned wholesale kidnaping of Americans, including Marines and sailors.

In the meantime, the efforts to obtain a truce on the part of the Church were continuing. Bishop Alfredo Muller of Havana and Bishop Alberto Martin Villaverde of the Province of Matanzas sent word to Castro asking for an emissary to discuss a peaceful solution.

Amongst the endeavors for a peaceful solution proposed by Church dignitaries were: that the Cuban Episcopacy, interpreting the thought and sentiments of the majority of the Cuban people, believed it to be incumbent upon themselves to halt violence under which the political problems of the country were being debated. The Church did not believe that peace in the land, with the restoration of democratic rights, could be obtained through violence and bloodshed.

The Cuban Episcopacy stated that they would endeavor to obtain the following objectives:

(A) Maintenance of public order.
(B) Respect for the fundamental rights of citizens.

(C) Free electoral process with equal rights and guarantees for all political parties.

These objectives could be obtained through the formation of a broadly-based neutral government, whose members would not be permitted to run for elective office in the ensuing elections. Its constitution would be drawn up according to the Constitution of 1940 and it would hold powers in conformity with Articles 281 and 282 of that Constitution.

Under this plan the Episcopacy would assume the responsibility of proposing the person to be designated as Prime Minister of the Cabinet. The Episcopacy would recommend persons for the Cabinet but the selection of the Cabinet would be the responsibility of the Prime Minister. The Episcopacy was prepared to enlist the support of social and civic groups.

In an effort to co-ordinate all national opinion on the political conflict church dignitaries were prepared to visit the President of the Republic to notify him of the endeavors to be realized. The Church was prepared to notify the Castros of their endeavors and also prepared to notify the leading representatives of the revolution in the United States.

From the Castros and from the representatives of the revolutionaries in the United States the Episcopacy would try to obtain written expressions, in the shortest period of time, of the proposals believed by each of them to be necessary to arrive at a peaceful solution to the national quarrel.

Once the opinions requested were obtained, the Episcopacy would incorporate them where compatible with a formula for the restoration of peace with democratic rights.

The Church was prepared to carry the ball by itself, but even the Cuban Episcopacy could not bring about a peaceful solution without the support of the United States. (The efforts of the Church by itself were not sufficient, as the Church carried less weight in Cuba than in other Latin American countries.) The Department was not willing actively to support any propositions for a peaceful solution. The reason given was that any such active support would be considered as intervening in the internal affairs of Cuba. Actually, we were consistently intervening in our day-to-day actions to bring about the downfall of the Batista dictatorship and to turn the government of Cuba over to Fidel Castro.

Before the United States Senate Sub-Committee to Investigate the Communist Threat Through the Caribbean I testified as follows on August 30, 1960:

> Because Batista was the dictator who unlawfully seized power, American people assumed Castro must, on the other hand, represent liberty and democracy. The crusader role which the press and radio bestowed on the bearded rebel blinded the people to the leftwing political philosophy with which even at that time he was already on record.
>
> [Castro's] speeches as a student leader, his interviews as an exile while in Mexico, Costa Rica, and elsewhere clearly outlined a Marxist trend of political thought.
>
> The official United States attitude toward Castro could not help but be influenced by the pro-Castro press and radio; certain members of Congress picked up the torch for him.

In response to a question from Senator Eastland regarding who was principally responsible for Castro's rise to power, my testimony went on as follows:

> Mr. Smith: Without the United States, Castro would not be in power today. I will put it as straight as that to you, sir.
>
> Senator Hruska: But the responsibility for that is a composite thing?
>
> Mr. Smith: [It] is a composite, that is correct.
>
> Senator Hruska: There may have been certain quarters in which there were more virulent advocates than others, but, just the same, it is a composite thing. Without that composite nature, very likely, the result which did follow may not have happened.

(*134*)

Mr. Smith: That is correct. In other words, I do not think it is fair to say that this individual or that individual or that particular agency, in itself, per se, is responsible for Castro coming to power. It is the composite.

Senator Eastland: The composite of the United States Government, is that it, and its branches?

Mr. Smith: Composite of those elements that formed the United States Government.

Senator Eastland: That formed the United States Government.

Mr. Smith: I mentioned segments of the press, certain members of Congress, the CIA, the State Department. All of them took a hand in this, Senator.

Senator Dodd: But in any composite picture, I think we all recognize that there are some influences that are stronger than others. They are never all the same.

Mr. Smith: No. Some must share a greater part of the guilt than others.

Senator Dodd: And some can do more than others.

Mr. Smith: And some are in a position to do much more.

Senator Dodd: That is what I think we are driving at.

Senator Eastland: And the agencies of the United States Government could do, of course, more than members of Congress or the press or anyone else.

Mr. Smith: That is true. You have all sorts of agencies.

Senator Dodd: Certainly, you can say it the other way. You can say that without the United States Government, the other factors of the composite picture could not do anything. If the government had stood firm and said, "We will not assist Castro," the fact that there were many other elements of our society who were sympathetic to him could not have brought it about, isn't that true?

Senator Hruska: Conversely, if the other elements—and I take what we would consider exterior elements; let's take business and the press—for example, had the press, in its opinion-making power, been antagonistic toward Castro, no amount of formal governmental action could have overcome that massive factor.

Mr. Smith: That is true.

Senator Hruska: The same thing is true with reference to im-

plementing Castro. If and when business located and having investments in Cuba would either by blackmail or by so-called taxes support financially the Castro movement, that was something which,
likewise, would be very helpful to those who in formal government
circles would say, "Let us also help Castro."

Mr. Smith: Those who paid tribute at the end were doing it
for their own self-protection because they felt that if they did not
do it they were going to lose their holdings.

Senator Eastland: As a matter of fact, now, wasn't it the impartiality of the United States Government that brought Castro to
power?

Mr. Smith: Wasn't it the impartiality?

Senator Eastland: Yes.

Mr. Smith: Senator, we are responsible for bringing Castro in
power. I do not care how you want to word it.

In the spring of 1958 some of the American press carried
exaggerated stories depicting chaotic conditions and violence
in the streets of Havana. The flow of tourists to Havana began
to dwindle to almost nothing. Hotels were empty. In the night-
clubs and the casinos the orchestras played to the waiters.

I cite one incident to describe the atmosphere of fear.

April 16, opening day for the baseball season, was approaching. The directors of the International League on April
13 voted to open the baseball season in Havana as scheduled,
but the Buffalo team sent word it would not show up because
of the stories carried in the press regarding the chaotic conditions in Havana.

I was able to reassure officials of the International League,
also officials of the Cuban, Buffalo, and Rochester clubs that
most of the violence was in faraway Oriente Province—more
than 600 miles from the Cuban capital.

"The shift in Buffalo's decision came after a talk between
the Buffalo team representatives and the American Ambassador to Cuba, Earl E. T. Smith," according to the *Miami Herald*
of April 16, which went on to say that "Ambassador Smith of

Havana assured the Buffalo team that 'conditions are normal in Havana'" and added, "If children can play in the streets of the city, why can't grown up men play in the stadium?"

The Buffalo team was given police protection during their four-day stay in Havana. A car carrying four military detectives followed the Buffalo team on its trips to and from the stadium —and on the trip to the airport when they left. On opening night, two detectives sat on the Buffalo players' bench. "With all that protection," the manager said, "I don't believe we were ever in any real danger."

The Buffalo, New York, *Courier Express* of April 21 wrote that the Buffalo Bisons arrived in Miami after completing operation Havana and that the general feeling among the athletes was that the Cuban political situation "has more bark than bite" as far as Americans were concerned. The *Courier Express* went on to say that each of the four games played in Havana were free of incidents.

President Batista purchased from the United States fifteen training planes to be used by the Cuban Air Force for the training of pilots. The planes were shipped to Fort Lauderdale, Florida, for delivery to Havana. Although the training planes had been bought and paid for and the Batista government had assured us that these planes would be used for training purposes only, their delivery was stopped by the Fourth Floor.

It was difficult to justify to the government of Cuba our refusal to deliver non-combat equipment. I again cabled the State Department that the only ones who would eventually benefit from our policy were the Communists. Finally, delivery was cleared by Deputy Assistant Secretary of State for Latin American Affairs, William Snow, over the objections of William Wieland. I was instructed to notify the government of Cuba that the fifteen training planes would be delivered.

I telephoned the Presidential Palace immediately to give this news to the President, who was presiding over a Cabinet meeting. This was good tidings for Batista, as the news helped mitigate the qualms of the Cabinet officials regarding the hostile pressure being applied by the United States.

The planes were never delivered. Shortly thereafter forty-seven Americans were kidnaped by Raúl Castro. The kidnaping of the Americans was used as an excuse by the Fourth Floor of the State Department to obtain a reversal of the decision to honor our commitment on the grounds that delivery of the planes might cause Raúl Castro to inflict bodily harm on the kidnaped Americans. I informed President Batista that delivery would only be suspended until such time as the kidnaped Americans were released. When the kidnaped Americans were eventually released, the State Department remained adamant in their refusal to make delivery.

For approximately three months the government of Cuba persisted in their requests for delivery. The actual possession of fifteen training planes in itself was not so important to the government; what was important was the psychological effect the refusal of delivery had upon the morale of the armed services and government officials. The State Department refused to grant permission to have the planes released from Fort Lauderdale but they did send a bill for storage and servicing facilities to the government of Cuba.

The reason given for refusal of delivery was the fear that bombs could be put on the planes—even though they were designed strictly for training purposes. This was a little far-fetched. You could use the same argument against the shipment of automobiles where machine guns might be mounted.

The Chief Counsel of the Committee on the Judiciary of the United States Senate inquired at the hearing:

Mr. Sourwine: You spoke of the fifteen training planes which were held up and I understood you to say they were held up because this government feared that if they were sent, there might be some harm to the kidnaped Americans?

Mr. Smith: That is correct.

Mr. Sourwine: Did you mean by this that the government of the United States was yielding to blackmail?

Mr. Smith: No, I do not think the United States Government was yielding to blackmail, but I think the State Department did not want to take any action which might help the Batista government and receive the protests of the revolutionaries.

Mr. Sourwine: Are you saying then that this was simply an excuse which was given?

Mr. Smith: I believe the Department was happy to have a reason to justify reversing their decision.

Our failure to deliver the twenty armored cars and our failure to deliver the fifteen training planes were an embarrassment to me. In both instances I was instructed to promise delivery. In both instances we failed to live up to our promises. Yet it is not fair to blame the State Department entirely for failure to deliver arms and military equipment to the Cuban government. Severe pressure was brought to bear on the State Department by members of Congress, the press, representatives of the revolutionaries in the United States, and American public reaction.

Chapter XV

The Communist Pattern

ON JUNE 22, Raúl Castro issued Military Order Number 30 calling for the kidnaping of American citizens in the area under his control. This order, written in the Communist pattern, justified the act on the grounds that his forces were receiving intensive bombardment by government planes allegedly being refueled out of the United States Naval Base at Guantánamo Bay.

Five days elapsed between the time of the issuance of the military order and when the first American was kidnaped. If American intelligence sources had been aware of Military

Order Number 30 during that five-day period, the Embassy would have immediately taken action to warn and evacuate all Americans in the area under the control of Raúl Castro. Also the State Department would have been able to appeal to Fidel Castro through his Washington representatives to countermand Raúl Castro's order.

The first Americans to be kidnaped were from the Moa Bay Nickel Company mining area on June 27. Later twenty-seven United States Marines and sailors were captured aboard a Cuban bus while returning to the naval base from an outing in Guantánamo City. The total number kidnaped was fifty (forty-seven Americans and three Canadians).

As soon as the Embassy received word of the kidnaping, I telephoned our Consul in Santiago, Park Wollam, and instructed him to go up in the hills and contact the rebels. My instructions to Wollam were: To inform the rebels immediately that you have been instructed to obtain as soon as possible a report on the whereabouts and conditions of Americans presumably kidnaped by the Castro group. The United States government will determine its course of action following your reply to this inquiry which will be expected within twenty-four hours.

The question arose amongst my staff whether I was correct in ordering the American Consul to contact the revolutionaries, whom the government of the United States did not officially recognize. I realized that time was of the essence and that any delay would mean loss of contact with the rebels and might endanger American lives. This was an occasion when an on the spot decision had to be made without delay. I was happy to receive a telephone call the following day from Allan Stuart, Deputy Chief of MID section, that my action had been approved after consultation with the legal division.

The rebels had swooped down from their mountain hideouts and kidnaped nine American and two Canadian engineers from the Moa Bay Mining property. They seized food and medical supplies and retired to the hills with their hostages. Consul Wollam, in accordance to his instructions, flew to Moa Bay from Santiago and walked into the foothills where he made contact with the rebels. His prompt appearance caught them unawares. He was able to impress on the rebels that the United States would not be blackmailed, would pay no ransom and demanded immediate and unconditional release of the captives.

President Batista ordered the Cuban Air Force to desist from bombing and strafing operations and ordered all armed forces to avoid military activity in the area.

With the permission of President Batista, Admiral R. B. Ellis, Commandant of the Naval Base at Guantánamo Bay, sent United States fighter aircraft on reconnaissance flights over the area with the purpose of frightening the rebels. On June 29, Vice-Consul Wiecha proceeded into the hills to the rebel hideout to make contact with the second group of rebels who had kidnaped thirty United States Marines and sailors.

A letter was received at the Embassy addressed to me from a small group of the captives, stating that they would be released under the following conditions: that we would cease the shipment of all military equipment to the government of Cuba; that we would cease servicing Cuban government aircraft with fuel out of the Guantánamo Naval Base; and that the United States would send a representative to the government of Cuba to obtain assurance that the government of Cuba was not using American military equipment in their campaign against the Castro forces.

The facts were: the State Department was not supplying arms to the Cuban government. The Guantánamo Naval Base was not fueling or servicing Cuban military aircraft. These charges were unfounded and were immediately denied by a press release from the State Department and from the Embassy in Havana.

Raúl Castro's decision to kidnap the Americans, in the Embassy opinion, was inspired by the following reasons:

(A) To obtain world publicity.

(B) To regain prestige, which the Castro forces lost as a result of the failure of the general strike.

(C) To force the government Air Force to cease bombing the rebel area.

(D) To try and gain public recognition from the United States.

To improve the uncertain radio communications between Oriente and Havana, I dispatched an Embassy plane with Second Secretary Bowdler to shuttle between the Guantánamo Base, Santiago, and Moa Bay. Bowdler was able to make constant reports to the Embassy through short wave radio communications which were set up between the Embassy, the Base at Guantánamo and the American Consulate at Santiago.

When Fidel Castro was contacted by rebel representatives in the United States by radio via Caracas, he insisted that the order for the kidnapings had been issued without his prior knowledge or approval.

I was instructed by the State Department to approach President Batista with the request that our Consul, Park Wollam, be permitted to fly in a Navy helicopter to the Sierra Cristal to pick up Raúl Castro and then proceed to the Sierra Maestra for an interview with Fidel Castro regarding the release of the captives.

Batista turned down this request, stating: As Chief of State I could not permit such a publicity stunt, primarily because I could not insure the safety of the American Consul or the American plane.

In Washington the Department continued to press for the release of the Americans through their numerous contacts, through Betancourt, the official rebel representative, and other revolutionary representatives in Washington.

President Batista was in a dilemma. He could not dislodge Fidel Castro and his followers from their hideouts. On the other hand he was under considerable pressure from the United States to obtain the release of the hostages. Batista, in my opinion, would have granted permission to land American Marines to release the captives.

The Navy Department, members of Congress and many of the top officials in Washington, as well as myself, were in favor of obtaining the approval of President Batista to land Marines to free the captives, if Raúl Castro did not immediately effect their release.

However, Assistant Secretary of State Rubottom's recommendation prevailed. He was against the landing of Marines on the grounds that we might only obtain the return of dead American bodies.

In my judgment, Raúl Castro would not have dared harm any of the kidnaped Americans. Even if he did not realize that the 26th of July revolutionary movement could not succeed without the sympathetic assistance of the United States, it was obvious that the landing of American Marines to free the Americans and Canadians would align the United States against the Castros. The wanton seizure of Americans and Canadians was an act repugnant to every standard of civilized conduct.

The rebels issued an ultimatum on negotiations to me. The ultimatum said the rebels would release all captive Americans as well as the Canadians only if I agreed to talk to Raúl Castro. This was turned down as were all of their demands. "Belligerent Status" was envisaged by the rebels, but never granted.

The Embassy never lost contact with the rebels. We were able to set up direct radio communication. A special operator with short wave equipment was flown from the United States by Central Intelligence to set up radio communications between the rebel hideout area and the Embassy in Havana.

I dispatched Eugene Gilmore, Counselor for Economic Affairs, by air to the United States Naval Base for a meeting with the Base Commander, Rear Admiral R. B. Ellis, in connection with the Americans and one Canadian still held as hostages by the Cuban rebels. Eugene Gilmore was a scholarly, serious, and highly intelligent Foreign Service Officer. At the same time Embassy Havana denied that Eugene Gilmore's trip had any connection with reports that the rebels wanted some high level negotiator to talk with them before releasing their remaining captives.

Due to the proximity of the Guantánamo Naval Base to our Consulate in Santiago and to the area where the kidnaped Americans were held, the Navy was able to give us valuable co-operation and aid through their facilities.

By July 2 we received word through our special operator in the rebel territory that the rebels were prepared to release seven Americans. To obtain full publicity, the rebels stipulated that a Navy helicopter be dispatched to the area. Four American citizens and a Canadian national were flown to the United States Naval Base. We still had forty-five more to be released. Consul Wollam assured me, after being freed himself and bringing back the five released hostages, that all remaining captives were well.

The captives were doled out in driblets. Four days later five additional civilians were released unharmed. The rebels were hanging on to the American hostages as long as possible because they enjoyed their respite from the Cuban Air Force bombings and strafings. Release of the servicemen was delayed to the end. Not until the middle of July were all released unharmed and flown out safely by helicopter.

From the interrogation of the kidnaped servicemen at

Guantánamo and from the interrogation of kidnaped civilians at the Embassy, it was learned that the idea of the kidnaping was inspired and originated in the minds of Raúl Castro and a bearded man known as "Buffalo Bill" (he was not known by any other name and some of the returned hostages said he was a Communist).

The Communist infiltration of the movement was also indicated through the violent anti-Americanism which was evident throughout the rebel leadership. Two of the top leaders of the Castro movement, Major Ernesto (Che) Guevara and Major Raúl Castro, belonged to Marxist organizations. The State Department knew that both had made extended visits behind the Iron Curtain. Both the CIA and the Department of State were aware that Che Guevara was an active Communist in Guatemala and Mexico and that Raúl Castro had been active in the international Communist student movement.

In the hills, Raúl Castro's girl friend, Vilma Espín (now Mrs. Castro), held nightly political discussions with the American prisoners. You could not get through to her because she was dedicated to the Communist technique of the big lie, reported some returned hostages. Yet influential individuals in the United States still refused to believe that the Castro movement was Communist-infiltrated and Communist-controlled.

These same persons now claim "the revolution has been betrayed" and "the revolution has devoured its children." [1] Raúl Castro evidently enjoyed the kidnapings because three months later, in October 1958, he kidnaped two more Americans and several Cuban employees of the Texaco Company.

I instructed Consul Wollam to contact the rebels and to tell them that unless they immediately released the Americans, I would recommend to the Department that we renew shipment of arms to the government of Cuba. I knew such recom-

[1] State Department White Paper on Cuba, April 1961.

mendation would go unheeded, because I was already on record with the State Department as advocating the sale of arms to the government of Cuba. However, the Castro people were not aware of this and I was convinced a firm approach was the only way to obtain results. Through their contacts with rebel representatives in Washington, the State Department tried to impress upon the revolutionaries the foolishness and gravity of their actions.

We did obtain results. The Americans were released three days later unharmed.

Cuban rebels coupled their kidnaping of two American oil company workers with a threat to kidnap British diplomats. The Rebels said they would abduct the diplomats in reprisal for British sale of arms to Batista's government.

On October 28, 1958, the following editorial "Sick and Tired" appeared in the *New York Journal American*. It was indicative of the reaction of the conservative press in the United States.

We are beginning to get the impression that Fidel Castro, the Cuban rebel leader, considers kidnaping American citizens an act of playful diplomacy that ought to be greeted with tolerant amusement in this country.

He has another think coming. Last year, Castro's guerrillas kidnaped 47 Americans. It was three weeks before all were released. Last week, two Americans were seized. They were freed two days later after our Ambassador, Earl E. T. Smith, sent Castro a stiff note by courier. State Department spokesman, Lincoln White, said the United States might have to take action unless these outrages were stopped.

Castro now calls these statements "aggressive declarations." He accuses Ambassador Smith of plotting with President Batista to provoke American intervention. In the light of Mr. Smith's efforts to lean over backward to be neutral in the Batista-Castro struggle, this is insulting nonsense.

The Castro attitude is a combination of arrogance and stupidity.

It is he who has committed aggression against American citizens.

It is he who has done the provoking.

We have no admiration for the Batista regime. But Castro is taking the most effective way to destroy whatever sympathy exists for his course. When a Washington official said, "We're sick and tired of having Americans kidnaped," he was speaking for all of us.

Before the sub-committee of the United States Senate I testified:

The revolutionaries under Fidel Castro demanded tribute throughout Cuba. By the fall or late summer of 1958, they also decided to demand tribute from American business and American property holders.

As soon as I heard this, I wrote a letter to every American business in Cuba in which I clearly stated that Americans should not pay tribute, and I asked them not to give any money to the revolutionaries, that we were still doing business with a friendly government, and that as Americans we had no right to pay money to active revolutionaries who were trying to overthrow a friendly government by force.

This letter was approved by the State Department before it was sent out. Every week I regularly had a meeting, in my Embassy, of some of the leading businessmen in Havana, and they assured me that the Americans were not paying money.

However, toward the closing days of the Batista regime, I believe some Americans did pay protection money. They were paying taxes to the Batista government and were also paying taxes to the Castro people. I couldn't prove it. They [wouldn't] let me know.

The Castro rebels demanded a loan of $500,000 from the Texaco Corporation, which the company firmly refused to make. When demands for tribute were made upon Americans, my letter was often used as an excuse for refusal. By the late summer there was practically a complete disregard on the part of the rebels for American lives and property.

Shortly after the kidnaped Americans were returned, the United States landed 3,500 Marines in Lebanon. This not only diverted public attention from Cuba but restored, to many of us, our national pride.

In the fall of 1958, the Secretary of State, John Foster Dulles, attended a dinner in his honor given by the Cuban Ambassador to Washington, Nicolas Arroyo. Such action did not indicate unfriendliness on the part of the top echelon of the State Department to the government of Cuba. It contrasted sharply with the attitude of those on the Fourth Floor and it caused much concern to the Castro sympathizers.

Near Moa Bay was the $100,000,000 American government's Nicaro Nickel plant where many Americans were employed. Washington decided to evacuate approximately fifty-five women and children who were dependents of American employees at the plant. The decision was based on a desire to provide extraordinary precautions for these Americans against possible harm by the rebels.

The US Attack Transport, *Kleinsmith,* was dispatched to Nicaro on the northern coast of eastern Cuba. In all, approximately fifty-five dependents of the American plant personnel were removed from Nicaro to the United States Naval Base on the southern coast. The remainder refused to leave. The Americans had been isolated in the rebel-infested area around the nickel plant. The huge aircraft carrier, *Franklin D. Roosevelt,* was ordered by the Navy Department to patrol the coast just outside the harbor to insure safety of the operation. At the time, I issued a statement that the decision to send the aircraft carrier to Nicaro was made in Washington and I emphasized the point that the presence of the carrier was merely to provide helicopter airlift in case such action were needed. All the dependents were safely evacuated to the naval transport.

The State Department through its spokesman, Lincoln White, said that the United States might have to take action if rebel kidnaping of Americans did not stop. The rebel leader countered by charging Batista and myself with plotting to provoke United States intervention. The charge against me apparently stemmed from the evacuation at Nicaro. When the evacuees arrived in Miami via the United States Naval Base at Guantánamo Bay, they reported that the rebels had held the town from four to five days during which time "we were definitely prisoners but the rebels didn't have much to say to us."

On October 25, 1958, Fidel Castro, in a personal broadcast from the Sierra Maestra Mountains, warned the United States to stay out of Cuba's rebellion. He was apparently referring to the State Department's statement that the rebel kidnapings were "uncivilized conduct." Castro said it was for the Cuban people, not the United States State Department, to pass on his actions.

On November 1, 1958, the registered agent in Washington for the rebel 26th of July Movement, Ernesto Betancourt, accused me and two United States generals of "conniving to undermine" the State Department's hands-off policy toward the Cuban civil war, according to the *New York Herald Tribune* of November 2, 1958.

The accusation was made by Betancourt in a letter to Senator Wayne Morse, Chairman of the Senate Foreign Relations Sub-Committee on Latin-American Affairs. According to the complaint, an American four-star general and an American two-star general, neither of whom he identified by name, wanted to see the United States support the fight of Cuban president, Batista, to put down the revolt. The *Herald Tribune* went on to say that Mr. Betancourt contended in his letter to Senator Morse that "it is obvious that United States Ambassador Smith, instead of faithfully following the policy established by his superiors, is conniving with this faction in the American military to undermine the State Department policy."

On November 2 Castro continued his wanton disregard of American life and property by ordering his gunmen to highjack another Cubana airliner. This time there were seven Americans aboard. Survivors reported that four Cuban rebels commandeered the big Viscount turbo-prop aircraft on a flight from Miami to Veradero Beach. The plane was forced to crash land in Nipe Bay near Preston in rebel territory in Oriente Province. I immediately dispatched two Consular representatives to Preston to make investigations at the scene and to identify the American dead so that the Embassy could immediately make a full report to the Department of State.

Although Señor Betancourt denied that the 26th of July Movement's Committee in exile in Miami had any connection with any of the men aboard the aircraft, survivors indicated to the contrary. Also, 26th of July Movement armbands were found amongst the wreckage.

This was another publicity stunt on the part of Castro. He seized the plane to make headlines. This was the second plane seized in flight since October 21.

On that date, two rebels among the passengers seized a DC3 with twelve others aboard. Two Cuban rebels, posing as passengers, captured a Cuban commercial aircraft while in flight over Oriente Province. They forced the crew at pistol point to land on a rebel airstrip in the Sierra Maestra Mountains.

Chapter XVI

The Elections That Failed

THERE WERE NUMEROUS PARTIES and numerous candidates in Cuba who belonged to the political opposition. These were members of what I termed the "legal opposition." Such groups took no part in terroristic activities. The political opposition was interested in the replacement of the government of Cuba through the normal processes of election and was not interested in the overthrow of Batista by violence.

On January 14, 1958, after a luncheon with President Batista, the leaders of the four government coalition parties announced that they would join together in proclaiming the government coalition candidate. The announcement was made through Justo Luis Pozo, the Mayor of Havana and leader of Batista's Progressive Action Party (PAP). The smaller parties to join with the PAP were the Democratic Party, the Liberal Party and the Radical Union Party. Their coalition candidate, selected by Batista, was former Prime Minister Andrés Rivero Aguero.

There were three main opposition parties: the Free Peoples Party (PL) whose Presidential candidate was Dr. Carlos Marquez Sterling; the Auténtico Party (PRC) whose Presidential candidate was ex-President of Cuba, Dr. Ramón Grau San Martin; the National Revolutionary Party (PNR) whose Presidential candidate was Pardo Llada.

Dr. Carlos Marquez Sterling wanted the opposition to consolidate behind one candidate—the same as the pro-government parties. Obviously, such a coalition would be much more effective than having the opposition split, while the government political parties were united and well organized. I was hopeful that the political opposition would agree to this objective. However, it was not possible to obtain such a coalition because of the opposition of the Auténtico Presidential candidate, former President of Cuba, Dr. Grau San Martin. The government candidate was not well known. But divided, the opposition had little chance to win.

As American Ambassador, the correct procedure was to have an "exchange of views" with each one of the leading Presidential candidates. The leaders of the two main opposition parties, Dr. Carlos Marquez Sterling and Dr. Grau San Martin, maintained until election day that free and open elections were the only solution to the Cuban political problems. But such elections must be held under the restoration of constitutional guarantees.

In early 1958, the Auténtico Party, whose Presidential candidate was Dr. Grau San Martin, and Dr. Marquez Sterling, of the Free Peoples Party, issued a Resolution calling for a truce in Cuba; asking for political amnesty and asking for a government of national unity. The Auténtico Party went on to say that it would encourage the registration of its political followers so they could vote and would continue to take the necessary legal steps required during the pre-election period.

The third opposition party, the National Revolutionary Party, whose leader was José Pardo Llada, suffered from disunity and the prolonged absence of its leader. As a result it dissolved before election day. At one time, Dr. Marquez Sterling unsuccessfully approached Pardo Llada to see if his party would be interested in having him (Dr. Marquez Sterling) as Presidential nominee for both parties.

The political parties completed the preliminary phases of the electoral processes and selected their national candidates. This was done in spite of Fidel Castro's ultimatum that any candidate running for office would be imprisoned or executed by his forces. On October 10, 1958, Fidel Castro issued, in the Sierra Maestra, the so-called Revolutionary Law Number Two, which called for capital punishment for all candidates to public office. He made no distinction between candidates for the opposition and candidates for the government. Castro announced over the rebel radio that "a candidate to any electoral post who is captured in the operations zone of the free territory will be given a sentence varying, in accordance with the degree of responsibility, between ten years imprisonment and death."

One candidate, Senor Anibal Vega, brother of the President of the Free Peoples Party in the province of Camaguey, was executed in this way. It was also Castro's orders to shoot and machine gun the citizens in line at the polling places on election day. Many local candidates were forced to resign.

In our many meetings, Batista had solemnly promised that he would hold honest elections. He also had promised that he would invite observers to witness the elections from the United Nations, the Organization of American States, and the world press. In October, the President did transmit to the United Nations a request from one of the opposition candidates, Dr. Grau San Martin, that the United Nations send observers. The Cuban delegate to the United Nations, Dr. Emilio Núñez Portuondo, transmitted this invitation. On behalf of the Batista government, he also extended a similar invitation to the United Nations to send observers to the elections. Also an invitation to the world press to witness the elections was issued by the government at the end of October.

In spite of Castro's threats and all-out effort to prohibit the general elections, the elections took place according to schedule on November 3. Election day was quiet. In Oriente, the rebels were successful in keeping the people from the polls. In the remaining Provinces, there was a substantial turnout. Official returns showed a turnout of approximately 60 percent.

Dr. Andrés Rivero Aguero, Batista's candidate, won. Dr. Marquez Sterling, the Free People's candidate, was second. In his platform, Dr. Marquez Sterling promised, if elected, to summon immediately a constituent assembly to shorten his mandate and to call for new elections. The Autentico candidate, Dr. Grau San Martin, trailed third.

Election night I received a phone call from Dr. Gonzalo Guell. From the conversation I gathered he was in the presence of Batista. When asked what I thought of the returns I was noncommittal, but my disappointment was keen. Election returns indicated that the results would not be acceptable to the people.

Batista's failure to live up to his solemn promise to me that he would hold free and open elections acceptable to the people was his last big mistake. If Batista's picked candidate had lost and if the election had been acceptable to the people a peaceful solution might still have been possible. As a result of the elections he lost whatever followers he had left. The people were now completely disillusioned and disappointed. They had hoped, up to the last, to find through elections a solution to the violence and civil strife.

If Dr. Marquez Sterling had won the election it would have removed from Castro his alleged goal to rid Cuba of Batista. Castro was fully aware of this fact. As a result, he was delighted when Batista's picked candidate won the general elections of November 3, 1958.

Dr. Marquez Sterling informed me that on various occasions he was approached by Castro representatives to obtain his withdrawal as a Presidential candidate. In his own words, "I always stubbornly refused to play the Castro line; maintained that Castro was a Communist working with the Communist Party to wipe out once and forever all democratic institutions from Cuba."

Dr. Andrés Rivero Aguero carried the provinces of Oriente and Las Villas where the vote was light as many people were afraid to come out of their homes to vote. Dr. Marquez Sterling won the provinces of Pinar del Rio, Matanzas, Havana and Camaguey. According to Dr. Marquez Sterling, he lost the election because of a changeover of the ballots. This is known in Cuba as *cambiazo*. Also Castro ordered his henchmen to burn and destroy the electoral documentation containing the ballots.

Dr. Marquez Sterling protested the election returns because the Free People's Party (PL) believed a recount would show they had won the Presidency. Dr. Roberto Melero presented an appeal, on behalf of the Free People's Party, to the Tribunal Superior Electoral, protesting the form of the count of the elections and demanding a complete recount.

The Tribunal Superior Electoral, which was created in the 1940 Constitution, did not have the opportunity to pass on the appeal. The Cuban Congress decreed that the electoral process was completed and the results final.

On Saturday, November 15, 1958, the President-elect, Dr. Rivero Aguero, lunched with me at the Embassy residence. His brother had been assassinated by the Castro revolutionists. I expressed my sympathy for his grief. He announced his desire to bring peace and tranquillity to the nation. He planned to convoke a constituent assembly, to shorten his mandate, to hold new elections and to restore full constitutional guarantees after February 24, 1959. Under these conditions, Dr. Rivero Aguero wanted to know if he could expect the support of the United States, which would include renewal of the sale of arms. The President-elect knew his cause was hopeless without American support. Dr. Rivero Aguero impressed me with the sincerity of his intentions to find acceptable terms for a peaceful solution of the political problems of the nation. Yet I doubted his ability to do so at this late date.

Chapter XVII

State Department Ambiguity

TO REMOVE the Rightist dictator, influential persons in the State Department were prepared to gamble on Leftist dictator control of the Castro movement. They were prepared to accept the assurances of the representatives of the revolutionaries in Washington that they would be able to control Castro.

Foreign Minister Guell informed me he knew on unimpeachable authority that William Wieland had stated that the United States would not intervene in Cuba until after there was chaos. Mr. Wieland allegedly went on to say that after there was a blood bath, the United States was prepared to call on the Organization of American States to obtain a mandate to restore order in Cuba. When I denied the charge Dr. Guell insisted he had the proof. I reported the conversation in December 1958, to the State Department. It was not denied.

Early in 1958 the State Department's own Bureau of Research and Intelligence conceded that at least one top leader (Che Guevara) was a Marxist and that there were reports of Communist infiltration. However, they did not believe the Fidelista Movement as a whole was Communist. In the summer of 1958, after the kidnapings, the Bureau of Research and Intelligence pointed out that the rebels were anti-American; that Communists had penetrated the lower ranks of the revolutionaries and admitted Communist sympathizers held top jobs in the movement.

In November 1958 an intelligence section of the State Department prepared an "Estimate Regarding the Communist Danger in Cuba." This report conceded that the 26th of July Movement was open to Communist exploitation and admitted the existence of Communist infiltration and the existence of Communist control of the revolutionary movement, but claimed they did not have sufficient evidence to determine the degree of control.

The corruption of the Batista government had sickened the Cuban people. They wanted a change. Batista had sown the seeds. Castro volunteers, aided by the Communist overt propaganda organs, used every conceivable facility to play up the strong-arm methods which existed. Off and on for eighteen years, Batista had played the dominant role in the government of Cuba, but now his government was disintegrating from within. The speed of this decomposition had been hastened by those many influences which carry weight in the United States and which are dedicated to the overthrow of Rightist dictatorships.

I was convinced that it had become a fixed American

policy to oppose all Rightist dictators, even those favorable to the United States. This policy opened the door to Leftist dictators and to the Communist Party. It was clear that this was a dangerous gamble, as each Communist Party, in whatever country, is a political arm of Soviet Russia.

On November 23 I went to Washington for consultation with the Department. I informed the State Department of my belief in Dr. Rivero Aguero's desire and intention to work out a compromise and I recommended that the State Department honor the President-elect's appeal for our support, as this was the most promising alternative left for avoiding chaos in Cuba for the sole benefit of the Communists. Secretary Rubottom's and William Wieland's estimate of the situation was that there was no possible solution to the Cuban problem through United States aid to the Rivero Aguero government, as they did not think that any of the respected civil and military elements would associate themselves with the government of the newly elected President. Further, they did not want to support and stimulate an effort by the Church to stop the fighting. My request for support of the Dr. Rivero Aguero government was refused.

The purpose of my visit was to inform the State Department concerning the rapidly deteriorating economic situation in Cuba. It was now obvious, even to the diehards, that the Batista government could not last. When questioned at a meeting in Deputy Under Secretary of State Robert Murphy's office regarding my estimate of the situation, I said the economy of Cuba was disintegrating. The main arteries of transportation were being shut off. The important bridges on the Central Highway were being destroyed. It would appear the revolutionaries were receiving professional advice on how to destroy the main lines of communication and transportation.

Under Secretary Murphy asked my opinion as to whether

the Castro movement was Communist. My reply was substantially as follows:

If I may have a jury of twelve unbiased people I will be willing to put up $100,000 that I can convince all the members of the jury within twenty-four hours that the Castro movement is infiltrated and controlled by the Communists. If I am unable to convince the jury, the money may be donated to any charity stipulated by the State Department. The Communists are too smart to give us any one piece of all-conclusive evidence. I need twenty-four hours to explain the sources, significance, and consistency of the evidence which has built up in the past eighteen-month period. I am sure that after twenty-four hours the jury will be convinced.

There was no comment regarding my offer and the discussion continued regarding the economic conditions in the island. I went on to give my views and reasons as to why the Cuban situation had deteriorated so rapidly.

Shortly after I became the United States Ambassador to Cuba I formed a consultative group from the local American business community to meet at regular intervals with myself and the top officers of the Embassy. The exchange of views held at these meetings was very helpful to all concerned. The last meeting with this group was held thirty-one days before President Fulgéncio Batista fled Cuba. Naturally the question of American policy toward Cuba came up for discussion.

The unanimous view expressed by these businessmen was that the Cuban situation had declined very rapidly. The consensus was that Batista could not last through to the end of his term of office (which was to expire February 24, 1959) and perhaps not beyond January 1, 1959, unless the United States was willing to give all-out support. The support of the United States might now be too late. These views turned out to be truly prophetic.

The group went on record that the Castro movement was

Communist-dominated. The Esso representative, G. W. Potts, pointed out that a recent 26th of July Movement statement was extraordinarily similar to a statement issued by the Arbenz government in Guatemala. There was unanimous agreement that the triumph of the Castro movement would be followed by bloodshed similar to the bloody aftermath of President Machado's overthrow. The businessmen went on to say that it was inconceivable that the United States assist Castro; but, as it was probably too late to help Batista, the best alternative would be the support of a military-civilian junta; to stand silently by and let Castro triumph was not in the best interests of the United States and not in the best interests of Cuba. So the group recommended that the United States should promote and give full and actual support, including the shipment of arms, to a military-civilian junta. There were approximately eight representatives of the American business community at this meeting. The balance were out of town. These gentlemen believed that a junta would be more likely to enlist general support from the people of Cuba and would weaken Castro were it to include some of the representatives of the political opposition, representatives of the civic groups now supporting Castro, and some of the best elements of the government of Cuba. Batista was to be excluded.

When I forwarded their views to the Department, I requested that the views of these responsible businessmen should be taken into account and that we should not be a silent spectator but should influence events toward a peaceful solution to keep the Communist influence from further developing.

I also recommended that Batista should be persuaded to turn over the Presidency to Dr. Rivero Aguero as soon as possible; that we support the new administration after being assured that the President-elect had the full support of the military and upon his official announcement to form a national unity government embracing the respected elements of both the political and civic opposition. This would require the calling of a constituent assembly and the shortening of the President-elect's own mandate by calling for general elections and the restoration of constitutional guarantees. Dr. Rivero Aguero had already assured me of his intentions to fulfill all of the above requirements. In my message to the Department, I again stated that the Communists would be the only ones to profit if the United States continued to refuse to support any solution excluding Castro, because of our non-intervention policy, and that the United States might well have to intervene later for humanitarian reasons.

Chapter XVIII

The Removal of Batista

ON THANKSGIVING DAY of 1958, I was approached at the Havana Country Club by Dr. Mario Lazo, an eminent Cuban attorney and a graduate of Cornell University. Dr. Lazo told me that he had some very important information. From past experience I knew him to be intelligent, trustworthy, and dependable. He was strongly anti-Batista, but was fearful that Castro would be even worse for Cuba than Batista.

Dr. Lazo informed me a decision had been made between the CIA and the Department of State to send an emissary to Cuba to suggest to President Batista that he leave the country, and to talk to Batista about setting up a military junta. I could make no comment as this was all news to me. It is significant that the American Ambassador should first receive such important information from a Cuban gentleman, no matter how dignified the source.

I later found that Dr. Lazo's information was correct and that the Department of State and the CIA had come to the conclusion in November that Batista must leave Cuba. At that time it was considered advisable to have someone other than the American Ambassador contact President Batista. The plan was to have me come to Washington for consultation and to retain me there until after Batista had been approached. This would protect the Ambassador's position, as far as the Batista government was concerned, if the plan did not materialize. The State Department wanted to protect itself against charges of intervention, so they planned to use an emissary with no official connection with the government.

Accordingly, I was summoned to Washington for consultation on December 4. On Wednesday, December 10, I met in Under Secretary Robert Murphy's office with Assistant Secretary of State Roy Rubottom, Deputy Assistant Secretary of State for Inter-American affairs William Snow, William Wieland, in charge of Caribbean affairs, and the CIA liaison with the State Department.

At this meeting I was informed by Deputy-Under-Secretary Murphy that Batista was to be approached by someone with no official connection with the government, with the suggestion that he (Batista) absent himself from Cuba and appoint a military junta. Possible suggestions for the junta were General Cantillo, Colonel Barquin, General Sosa, and one other. My opinion was asked and I agreed that I had been convinced for some time that Batista should leave the country to avoid more and more bloodshed and, further, that I agreed to the plan in the hope that a military junta would be successful in setting up a provisional government excluding Castro, and later would hold general elections.

On that same night, December 10, I telephoned Under Secretary Murphy and asked if I could see him at his home. I went to his home to ask if the military junta was to be formed with the approval of Batista. Under Secretary Murphy told me that it was to be done with the approval of Batista; that Batista had been approached the day before, but he did not mention the name of the emissary or the outcome of the meeting. I was glad that the responsibility for Cuban affairs, even at this late date, was being turned over to Under Secretary Robert Murphy, for I never had anything but the greatest respect for this long-time career officer.

William D. Pawley, the secret emissary, testified before the sub-committee of the United States Senate Judiciary that he was the one selected to go to Cuba and talk to Batista, to see if he could convince him to capitulate. Pawley met with President Batista on December 9, 1958, and I quote from Mr. Pawley's testimony before the sub-committee of the United States Senate Judiciary on September 2, 1960:

> I was selected to go to Cuba to talk to Batista to see if I could convince him to capitulate, which I did. I spent three hours with him on the night of December 9.

> I was unsuccessful in my effort, but had Rubottom permitted me to say that "what I am offering you has tacit approval, sufficient governmental backing," I think Batista may have accepted it.

> I offered him an opportunity to live at Daytona Beach with his family, that his friends and family would not be molested; that we would make an effort to stop Fidel Castro from coming into power as a Communist, but that the caretaker government would be men who were enemies of his, otherwise it would not work anyway, and Fidel Castro would otherwise have to lay down his arms or admit he was a revolutionary fighting against anybody only because he wanted power, not because he was against Batista.

(*166*)

Senator Keating: And the new government would also be unfriendly to Castro?

Mr. Pawley: Yes.

Mr. Sourwine: Who would the new government have been?

Mr. Pawley: The men we had selected and that had been approved and that I could tell Batista were Colonel Barquin, Colonel Borbonnet, General Díaz Tamayo, Bosch of the Bacardi family, and one other whose name at the moment escapes me. But there were five men, all enemies of Batista.

It came within that close of working, and the only thing, in my judgment, that made it fail to work was to say—after all, I had known this man thirty years and I could talk to him frankly—"if you will do this it will have the approval of the American government."

All I could say to him was, "I will try to persuade the United States Government to approve."

Senator Keating: But they wouldn't let you say it, though?

Mr. Pawley: No, which was tragic in a way because I think it would have avoided the problem.

Mr. Sourwine: Did you know that six days after you saw Batista on the 9th of December the American Ambassador saw him and told him that the United States Government had lost confidence in his ability to keep peace and that to avoid bloodshed the best thing that could happen would be for him to leave the country?

Mr. Pawley: No, I did not know that, and had I been privy to that I would have done what I could to have prevented that from happening that way because that is—the only possible result of that would be Fidel Castro would have immediately come into power, and I am convinced that there was enough noise made in the meetings of the Department of State and in CIA for enough people to be convinced that Castro could bring us nothing but disaster.

Mr. Sourwine: Do you have any knowledge respecting any information conveyed officially or on official orders to the newly elected government of Cuba, the Rivero Aguero government, that it would not have this support from the United States Government?

(167)

Mr. Pawley: No.

Mr. Sourwine: Do you have any knowledge of such an intelligence being communicated to Batista, that we would not support the Rivero Aguero government?

Mr. Pawley: No, I did not know that.

Dr. Mario Lazo on Thanksgiving Day, 1958, gave me the names of the individuals, representing certain American business interests, who were advised at a meeting in Washington by the Director of the Central Intelligence Agency that an emissary would be dispatched to Havana to discuss with Batista the possibility of his appointing a junta and absenting himself from Cuba. This leakage of information from a Cuban that an emissary other than the American Ambassador was to interview Batista, the President of the Republic, was embarrassing.

When I was in Washington on consultation, December 4-10, 1958, I disclosed to Secretary Rubottom all the detailed information I had received regarding the emissary to be dispatched to Havana and its disclosure to the American business executives. I asked him if he would or could confirm my information. His complete silence assured me of its veracity.

Although I knew Batista had been approached, I did not know the results, and I did not know the name of the individual who approached him. So, several days before my interview with the President of the Republic, I asked Secretary Rubottom, in a cable, to avoid being at a disadvantage, to advise me if Batista had been approached. There was no response.

Although it is true that the rebels never won a military victory and were only successful in seizing military outposts and in winning skirmishes, by December 1958 the will to resist on the part of the Cuban Army was rapidly vanishing. The Army would not fight. Desertions to the Castro rebels increased. The top command of the Cuban Army believed their cause was lost.

The situation throughout Cuba was crumbling. In Las Villas Province, Che Guevara and Camillo Cienfuegos were preparing to take the city of Cienfuegos. Cabaiguan reportedly was seized by the rebels, which meant that the central highway from Santa Clara east would be effectively shut off. The purpose was to cut the island in half. Early in December government fears that the rebels might successfully smash the communication lines in Las Villas were becoming factual. In addition to bridges being dynamited great stretches of the Central Highway were destroyed.

Batista planned to have transplanted from Osaka, Japan, a $10,000,000 small arms plant to manufacture rifles in accordance with American standards. All the details were arranged. The deal was never consummated because of financial difficulties.

Batista arranged and prepared the equipment of an armed train to carry technicians for reconstruction of the general transportation system. The idea was good, but the will to fight was gone. The train never was put in operation.

Castro's control of most of the country's transportation facilities in farmland areas threatened the 1959 sugar crop. The latest assessment of sugar leaders was that if conditions got no better or no worse, the 1959 crop would be less than four million tons. In Oriente Province the rebel blockade paralyzed most of the land and highway transportation. In the adjoining provinces of Camaguey and Las Villas, trains were running only intermittently.

In the early morning hours of December 14, I received my instructions from Washington. It was obvious, Assistant Secretary Roy Rubottom said, from the publicity attendant upon my last Washington conference and from statements being made by the government of Cuba, that President Batista still retained the highest hopes that the American Government would support Dr. Rivero Aguero, who had been elected on November 3, 1958. My task was to disabuse him of these ideas.

My instructions were clear, so I had immediately arranged for a meeting with the Foreign Minister, Dr. Guell. After the usual diplomatic and pleasant exchanges of greetings, I asked for an appointment with the President. "It is my unpleasant duty," I said, "to inform the President of the Republic that the United States will no longer support the present government of Cuba and that my government believes that the President is losing effective control."

After an understandable moment of silence, the Foreign Minister assured me the President would be pleased to see me within the next few days. He also assured me that he would try to prevail upon the President to act promptly in attempting still to develop acceptable measures to produce a viable solution. The Foreign Minister realized fully that extraordinary measures were necessary if the situation was to be resolved. Although he paled at my statements he remained calm. It is notable that throughout all of our many meetings where views were exchanged, no matter how unpleasant some were, I found the Foreign Minister to be understanding, sympathetic, cordial, and friendly.

So the moment had arrived to deliver my instructions from the State Department to President Batista. Driving along through the dark Cuban night, I realized that Batista and I had come to the end of the road in Cuba and that soon we would be faced with Castro.

The car was slowing down. I was aware we had arrived at my fateful destination. The American flags on the fenders shone brightly and briefly as flashlights in the hands of soldiers guarding the gates of Finca Kuquine were pointed first at the driver and then into the back seat, before we were waved on. The lights were lit throughout the grounds of the Finca. Here and there I could see tommygun-carrying soldiers walking through the grounds on patrol. The atmosphere was foreboding and sinister.

As the car passed the main house, proceeding on toward the small building in which Batista worked and maintained his library, I reviewed in my mind for the last time my instructions. The talk took place in the familiar, small private office where we had met on so many previous occasions. Only Dr. Guell was present throughout the two hour and thirty-five minute interview on the night of December 17, 1958. Once again, the meeting was conducted in a friendly and cordial atmosphere. The short powerfully built man, Fulgéncio Batista, who still exuded an air of strength to all outward appearances, sat apparently unfeelingly across the room from me. His face portrayed not the slightest sign of emotion, and his piercing dark eyes never left my face as we talked.

My entire premise was that the people of the United States had been bound to the people of Cuba for many years with affectionate ties of friendship; that we would not intervene in the internal affairs of Cuba; that we were motivated by humanitarian reasons to avoid more bloodshed from which only the Communists would be the beneficiaries; and that my government was further motivated by its hemispheric responsibilities and by our appreciation of Batista's many contributions to Cuban history. I spoke of our appreciation of the many acts of friendship for the United States demonstrated by him and of the historical neighborly bonds which had existed between our countries for so many years.

In detail, I explained to President Batista how I had tried to prevail upon the State Department on my last trip to Washington in early December 1958, to give some signs of support to the government of Cuba's plans for the ensuing administration under Dr. Andres Rivero Aguero. I had failed in my endeavor because my government was convinced that Batista had lost effective control of the situation.

I went on to tell the President that the Department of State was aware of his valuable past friendship and co-operation with the United States Government, and had arrived at this decision reluctantly. The State Department's estimate of the situation was that a crisis was impending which most likely would create prolonged civil disorders with much loss of life. If he would act promptly, the State Department still believed that there were Cuban elements which could salvage the rapidly deteriorating situation. It would be necessary to obtain their support and co-operation for a broadly based government, which would be capable of carrying out constructive measures for a national solution.

In accordance with my instructions, I conveyed to the President that the Department of State would view with skepticism any plan on his part, or any intention on his part, to remain in Cuba indefinitely. The President asked if he could come to Florida with his family to visit his home in Daytona Beach. I suggested Batista spend a year or more in Spain or some other foreign country and that he should not delay his departure from Cuba beyond the time necessary for an orderly transition of power.

President Batista countered that the army would disintegrate if he left the country. In his opinion the only workable solution was for Dr. Rivero Aguero, shortly before assuming the Presidency, to announce a coalition cabinet, formed from representatives of responsible elements; to announce the calling of a general assembly and that such national assembly would call for general elections, but that such assembly must have the full support of the United States, including the shipment of arms.

I further queried the President concerning his intentions about leaving Cuba. His answer was that the conditions at the time would be a determining factor. When I asked the President if he thought he could control the situation until February 24, when the new President-elect would take office, he said it would be difficult because the United States had refused him arms at his time of need.

In our meeting, I made it clear that I was not permitted to discuss any specific solutions or discuss personalities for a possible junta. I tried to convey to the President that all suggestions were made in a spirit of friendship and were made only because my government feared the situation had deteriorated to such an extent that his government could not survive very much longer. Yet I had to disabuse the President of any prolonged expectation that the United States would reinforce his position at the time. In addition, during our exchange of views, I was not permitted to hold up before him any prospect of appropriate United States backing for a solution which would have the genuine support of the people of his country.

I believe I accomplished all this and yet did not leave any impression that I, as American Ambassador, actively participated in any effort to select or establish a successor government.

The President raised the possibility of the formation of a military junta. He was of the opinion that no such junta could survive without his support and added that President-elect Rivero Aguero should be included in any contemplated solution. The President further stressed the point that if Castro took over the government he was absolutely sure that the United States would eventually be compelled to intervene because of the Communist control of the 26th of July Movement. The President discussed the possibility of President-elect, Dr. Rivero Aguero, immediately calling a constitutional assembly and having general elections as soon as the law would permit. He further suggested a broad coalition cabinet with representatives of the non-militant opposition elements. He also spoke of political amnesty after the cessation of all hostilities. As long as the Cuban Army had a constructive political pattern to support, he, Batista, could leave for Spain or Daytona Beach when this solution was in effect. Any viable solution, however, should include President-elect, Rivero Aguero.

The President asked if the United States would be willing to stop the fighting. When I replied that the American government could not intercede or mediate, he told me I was now mediating on behalf of the Castros.

For a man in his political death agonies Batista appeared outwardly placid; though I could not help but notice the sound of his breathing. He breathed like a man who had been hurt and both he and I knew he had. Batista stated that in the future it would be too dangerous for us to meet, as the subjects of our talks could only be beneficial to the Castros and tied his hands. A leakage would be fatal to his government. No one must know, not even the President-elect. He designated Foreign Minister Guell as our confidential liaison. The President accepted my comments in the same spirit in which they were given although I had dealt him a mortal blow. He said, in substance, "You have intervened in behalf of the Castros but I know it is not your doing and that you are only following out your instructions."

In my subsequent report to the State Department, I said I believed Batista would accept mediation to stop the fighting and that I further thought it was now incumbent upon the United States to seek some means to stop the fighting. I repeated it was my belief the Church would still go to any length to bring about peace if I could assure the Church of the United States support. My recommendation was that I be authorized to contact the Papal Nuncio and suggest that the Church set up an impartial committee to approach both Batista and Castro. I further recommended that the Organization of American States be approached to support mediation by the

Church. Otherwise my role was to sit in Havana and watch Batista's death throes.

For the United States to stand silently by meant there would be a period of chaos and bloodshed in Cuba, for the sole benefit of the Communists.

The Department of State was not receptive to any suggestions from Batista. The State Department did not believe that the constitutional transfer of power to the President-elect was the only way to keep the situation from further deterioration. I was further advised by Assistant Secretary Rubottom that the State Department did not wish to go along with any idea of supporting an effort by the Church to stop the fighting, because there were doubts as to whether the Church hierarchy would be effective in such an undertaking.

The day after my meeting with President Batista, the Prime Minister, Dr. Gonzalo Guell, requested an interview. He said President Batista wanted him to review our conversation of the previous day. The President wished to be doubly sure of the attitude of the United States. After confirming our conversation of the previous evening, I told the Foreign Minister that I could not prevail upon the State Department to support Batista's proposed solutions.

I left the Foreign Minister with a heavy heart for I knew that it was now too late to set up a government without Castro, especially if support from the United States was not forthcoming. When it was possible to set up such a provisional government without Castro and without Batista, the State Department had refused to lend its support on the grounds that such support would be deemed intervention. For twelve months, before the ship of state had foundered, there were occasions when a solution to the Cuban problem could have been obtained.

I recalled the unanimous view expressed by the representatives of the American businessmen in Havana at my last meeting with the consultative group on December 1, when they asked me to advise the State Department that the Castro movement is Communist-inspired and -dominated; that it was inconceivable that the United States assist Castro by silently standing by and permitting Castro to triumph. The United States had done more than stand silently by permitting Castro to triumph; the United States had diplomatically, but clearly, told the President of the Republic that he should absent himself from his country.

The gist of my exchange of views at the meeting with Batista on December 17, 1958, were publicly revealed through Batista's intimates early in 1960.

On March 19, 1960, the American press carried charges made by a former Cuban newspaper editor that I forced dictator Batista out of office. According to the United Press International, the charges came from a former Batista private secretary, Raúl Acosta-Rubio, who formerly published newspapers in Havana and Caracas. Contacted by newspaper reporters, I made the following comment: I am extremely interested in Mr. Acosta-Rubio's statement, but any comment should come from Roy R. Rubottom, Assistant Secretary of State in charge of Latin American Affairs.

On August 30, 1960, I verified the substance of my interview with Batista under oath before the Sub-Committee of the United States Senate on Internal Security. In this book is the first authentic detailed revelation.

The Air Force was still loyal to President Batista, and he was planning to go ahead with the military campaign in Las Villas Province in a last desperate attempt. If he was to retain control he knew he must rally the armed services and attack.

The State Department took the position that the United States could not actively support any solution which would not bring about the cessation of active hostilities. Time was running out and I informed Dr. Guell that we questioned the advisability of Batista sending his family to Florida. Because of the large pro-Castro Cuban population in Florida, my government would be concerned as to the safety of his family.

One week before Batista fled Cuba I received word through the military attaché that General Francisco Tabernilla y Dolz, Commander in Chief of the Cuban armed forces, requested an interview. General Tabernilla, accompanied by General del Rio Chaviano and General Carlos Tabernilla, arrived in their military police cars at the Embassy residence. General Carlos Tabernilla was the Chief of the Cuban Air Force. General Chaviano had been Commander in Chief of the armed forces in Oriente Province.

General Carlos Tabernilla and General Chaviano went to an adjoining room while General Francisco Tabernilla and I conferred alone. After General Tabernilla had described the seriousness of the situation, he said that some sort of solution should be brought about immediately in order to avoid Castro assuming power. General Tabernilla stated that the Cuban soldiers would not fight and that the government would not be able to survive much longer. He said that a military junta should immediately be formed, consisting of General Cantillo, General Sosa Quesada, Colonel García Casares, and a representative from the Navy. His idea was that all the top general staff should leave Cuba, and also those closely associated with President Batista. The General stated that the purpose of his visit to me was to save Cuba from chaos, Castro, and Communism.

General Tabernilla wanted to give Batista safe convoy out of the country. It was not to appear that Batista was leaving as a fugitive. It should appear as though the junta compelled him to leave. The junta would place Batista on the plane and call on Vice-President Guas Inclan to assume control. He wanted to know if the United States would support such a junta. I replied that I would report the conversation to the State Department, but that I did not believe that the State Department would send a direct reply for me to give him. I went on to say that if we should answer him directly it would be undermining President Batista, to whom I was the accredited Ambassador of my country. General Tabernilla understood this position and asked for guidance. My suggestion was that he go back and confer with the President. I asked General Tabernilla if he had mentioned his contemplated visit to me to President Batista, and he said, "No, I have not." He said, "I have not told him I was coming to see you, but I have discussed the problem in general with Batista."

I did not indicate in any way to General Tabernilla that Batista and I had already conferred.

General Tabernilla's thoughts were not clear. His plan was not practical. Some of the points were obscure. I believe the General was groping for help out of desperation.

I learned from General Tabernilla that the campaign in Las Villas would not be successful. He complained about the shortage of arms from which the government of Cuba was suffering. I could give the General no encouragement. Accompanied by the other generals, he left the American Embassy assuring me that they would see President Batista the same day and would recommend an exchange of views between Batista and myself.

It was obvious from this visit that the government of Cuba was about to fall apart. I notified Secretary Rubottom that if they were going to take any action at this late date, or had any further recommendations, such steps must be taken immediately.

Within one hour the phones at the Embassy Residence were ringing. My wife's friends wanted information regarding the visit of the generals, but she told them nothing. "Radio Bemba" was at work. The passing of information from one person to the other was called Radio Bemba in Cuba. It was not difficult to understand because, during the interview, the Embassy residence was surrounded with Army Intelligence police cars, and an Army helicopter hovered overhead.

As soon as President Batista heard of our interview he took steps to remove much of the authority of General Francisco Tabernilla. General del Rio Chaviano took off for Ciudad Trujillo the same evening to take asylum in the Dominican Republic.

Events had moved rapidly since my first approach to Batista, and it was becoming clear that events were now at a point where Batista could not exercise a satisfactory degree of control over the situation. If Batista were to start to negotiate with candidates for the junta, word would spread and such a leakage would be catastrophic for the Batista government.

From December 17, 1958, until Batista fled Cuba in the early morning hours of January 1, 1959, Dr. Guell and I continued to have daily meetings. From these conferences I knew that President Batista was aware of the extent to which his position had eroded. Batista's attitude about leaving Cuba had changed. He indicated a willingness to leave Cuba at that time rather than wait until after February 24, 1959, which was the date when President-elect Rivero Aguero was designated to take over the reins of the Cuban government.

On December 8, 1958, the State Department instructed United States Ambassadors to the Latin American Republics to obtain from the local governments their reactions to the Cuban problem. The purpose also was to determine which of the Republics would be willing to mediate. The replies received indicated varied reactions.

While I was having daily conferences with Dr. Guell, the State Department carried on consultations with several Latin American Republics. The purpose was to interest them in possible mediation in the Cuban conflict. A proposal was discussed to have several ex-presidents of American Republics lend their offices to mediate in the Cuban conflict for humanitarian reasons. Batista was fully informed of these consultations through his Embassy in Washington, D.C.

I had notified the State Department that there was a rapid deterioration in the economic and political situation of Cuba and that there was a very real danger the Communists would emerge in key positions.

I reported that Jorge García Montes believed that José Aguilera and Lazaro Pena would become the leaders of the Bank Employees Union and the Confederation of Labor, and that small farmers were being told that the land was theirs. Both Pena, who was in Mexico at that time, and Aguilera were believed to be affiliated with the Communists.

Jorge García Montes had held the office of Prime Minister longer than any other Prime Minister in Cuba. In the opinion of the Embassy he was a man of integrity and reliability. His opinions and his information were later borne out to be correct and reliable.

Dr. Gonzalo Guell informed me that Batista would be ready to leave Cuba as soon as the army was strengthened and the government stabilized. However, this would require United States support, including the shipment of arms.

It was Batista's belief that the plan with most chance for success was for President-elect Rivero Aguero, before February 24, to commence conversations for the forming of a national unity Cabinet to include the responsible elements of the opposition. The new Cabinet would call for general elections, and for the election of a National Assembly to draw up a new Constitution. The National Assembly would be sovereign.

To enable the government of Cuba to fight the Castros with success, the Cuban government insisted that such a plan would require the backing of the United States, including the supplying of arms.

The State Department replied there was no solution as long as Batista remained in Cuba. On the other hand, Batista considered the situation must be stabilized before his departure to avoid complete breakdown of public order.

I knew Batista's suggestions by now were hopeless. They were the requests of a dying government. The die had been cast. Yet I also knew that Castro would take over as soon as Batista left Cuba. In good faith I felt I must fight Castro's taking over the island to the bitter end. Perhaps I hoped for a miracle. With the help of the State Department, even at this late date, we might have performed a miracle.

With United States support there was still hope, remote as it might seem, that Dr. Rivero Aguero could enlist the support of the responsible opposition in the new provisional government. In any case, it was better to assume the risk than to have Castro obtain the reins of government; and I so advised the State Department.

I was instructed to call on Dr. Guell and inform him that the United States did not consider Batista's latest proposals to offer the likelihood of a workable solution; that these proposals signified merely the continuation of the present type of regime and policies without Batista, to be supported by United States arms. And I was further instructed to notify Dr. Guell that should the United States accept these proposals, it would result in charges of American military intervention in internal Cuban affairs. This would harden the attitude of many Cubans against the provisional government. It would also adversely affect the United States Latin American policy, with far reaching adverse consequences in the opinion of the Department of State.

I was authorized to tell Prime Minister Guell that the only prospect for a peaceful transfer of power was for Batista to select a transitional government of national unity. I was not authorized to suggest names of prospects to serve under such a plan. Batista did not believe that such a solution was workable. It was now too late. Batista sent word to me through Dr. Guell that if he were to approach anyone with the suggestion to serve on a new cabinet, the word would quickly spread, and the present government would collapse.

Any lingering hopes of keeping Castro from taking over the government of Cuba were rapidly dying. I was sure that soon we would be witnessing the third act of a Greek tragedy, and I so advised the State Department. It was apparent that nothing further could be done to change the course of events.

Desertions to the Castro rebels increased. Many of the high ranking officers were conspiring against the government. General Eulogio Cantillo was considering a plan to defect to Fidel Castro. If General Cantillo defected it would be the end of the Batista dynasty, for he was in command of the government's largest and best equipped battalions.

On Christmas Day, 1958, Dr. Guell came to the American Embassy with the news that he was leaving for Ciudad Trujillo the next day for a few days to repay a courtesy visit from the Dominican Foreign Minister. In the light of later events, many people have believed that Dr. Guell went to the Dominican Republic to prepare for the eventual flight of Batista to Ciudad Trujillo. In my opinion, this is not so. I believe Dr. Guell went to the Dominican Republic to discuss the shipment of arms from the Dominican Republic to Cuba. Arturo Espaillat and three other Dominican officials had arrived in Havana at that time, reportedly to discuss the stepping up of the shipment of arms from the Dominican Republic to the government of Cuba. According to the Prime Minister, Generalissimo Trujillo was glad to assist Batista by the shipment of arms, not because of any personal friendship for Batista, but because the Castros were fighting for the cause of Communism.

By this time Batista was ready to make any sacrifice to bring about a change of power in Cuba without the Castros, and the United States was in a position to dictate terms. Batista, through Guell, notified me he was open for discussion, and stated if the Cuban Army would receive immediate support, especially arms, to face Castro, he would immediately turn over the government to Vice-President Guas Inclan. If Inclan was not receptive to the offer he would turn over the government to the President of the Senate, Anselmo Alliegro, and that he, Batista, would leave Cuba immediately. All actions must be concurrent.

Batista asked that we accept his plan. He preferred that we should agree to turning over the government to Anselmo Alliegro rather than Guas Inclan because Inclan was to assume the office of Mayor on January 28, 1959, and it would be more complicated to turn over the presidency to him.

I was still making a last effort to keep out Castro so I recommended to Secretary Rubottom that the State Department agree to the forming of a new cabinet by either Rafael Guas Inclan or Anselmo Alliegro. The new cabinet must include responsible elements of the opposition. With the immediate departure of Batista, I stated the co-operation of responsible elements might still be obtained.

The alternative offer from Batista was to turn over the government of Cuba to President-elect Rivero Aguero immediately, but that the government of Cuba must receive backing from the United States, especially in terms of the shipment of arms.

Dr. Guell said that the government of Cuba could be turned over to President-elect Rivero Aguero legally by advancing the date for the new administration by the same legal procedure as it was established. However, no plan could succeed without the full support of the United States, and especially without the shipment of arms. Dr. Guell specified that the agreement must be made first and all steps be taken simultaneously; otherwise, according to Dr. Guell, the mobs would be in the streets and Castro would emerge the victor. If the United States had any alternative, feasible suggestions Dr. Guell asked that Batista be immediately advised.

If Cuba were to be saved from Castro, full support from the United States was required, but the State Department had no intention of going that far.

I inquired as to Batista's contemplated destination. Dr. Guell said that the President wanted to go to his home in Daytona Beach, Florida. In accordance with my instructions from the State Department, I suggested Spain. Dr. Guell asked if Batista's family could go to Daytona Beach if Batista went to Spain. I replied there would be no objections to this request.

On the morning of December 31, 1958, I sent my secretary, Edith Elverson, to inspect Dr. Guell's house as a possible tenant. Mrs. Guell was busily packing. The Foreign Minister and Mrs. Guell wanted to rent their home to an American, anticipating the looting of homes which would take place after they fled Cuba. It was hoped American occupancy would act as a deterrent to vandals.

On the same day, I informed Secretary Rubottom that President Batista, Foreign Minister Guell, and other government officials and their families would leave Cuba in the next twenty-four hours. This message informed Secretary Rubottom that Batista's family would leave for New York in the Presidential plane and that a stopover in Florida might be necessary to refuel. I also informed Secretary Rubottom in the same message that Batista himself was going to the Dominican Republic.[1]

It had been the custom for years for Batista to have a

[1] In the recently published *Cuba Betrayed* by Fulgéncio Batista, it would indicate that I was not aware of Batista's destination; however, my records are that I informed Secretary Rubottom of Batista's destination the day before his departure.

New Year's Eve party at Camp Columbia. This year he did not have the usual party; however, he did invite a few intimates, their wives, relatives, top government officials and chiefs of the military to come to Camp Columbia after dinner for a cup of coffee. Absolutely nothing was leaked of Batista's intention. There were about seventy who gathered that evening in a tense atmosphere and with little conversation. Both Andrés Domingo, Secretary to the President, and Dr. Gonzalo Guell carried large manila envelopes which never left their persons. No one knew what the contents were. But in the light of events since then, those present at the time now speculate the envelopes were full of American cash. Actually, they contained passports.

President Batista mingled among his guests with a few pleasant words for each one of them. He spent half his time in the reception room, where his intimates were gathered, and the rest of the time in an adjoining room obtaining last minute reports from the military chiefs as to the hopelessness of the situation. Little was said by the guests. The atmosphere was tense and foreboding, yet no one present suspected that the Batista dynasty was to end that evening.

At about 1:00 A.M. Mrs. Batista left the room, announcing that she was going to change her dress because she was feeling chilly. Shortly thereafter the guests left, not realizing that this would be the last time they would see their President.

After the guests had gone, former Prime Minister Jorge García Montes and the President-elect Dr. Rivero Aguero were informed for the first time of Batista's plans to leave Cuba. Both were invited to board the plane. Jorge García Montes declined the invitation, preferring to remain in Cuba.

At approximately 2:00 A.M. on January 1, 1959, Fulgéncio Batista resigned. A provisional government was designated in accordance with the Constitution of 1940. The oldest justice of the Supreme Court, Justice Carlos Piedra, was the next in line to assume the Presidency according to the Constitution of 1940. General Eulogio Cantillo was appointed Army Chief of Staff.

The President, the President-elect, the Prime Minister, the leaders of the armed services, heads of government, chiefs of police, their wives and children proceeded to the military airfield where three Cuban Army DC4's were standing by. They were to be flown by Cuban pilots of Cubana Airways. These young men knew nothing of their mission until they saw President Batista and his group boarding the planes. The pilots were not informed of their destination until they were airborne.

Batista, his wife, his son Jorge, Dr. and Mrs. Guell, Dr. Andrés Rivero Aguero and other government officials flew to Ciudad Trujillo, Dominican Republic. The other two planes left for the United States with Batista's other children and more of his close government collaborators. After Batista landed in the Dominican Republic he gave the pilot and co-pilot each $1,000 in cash.[2]

The Dominican government had no advance knowledge of Batista's arrival in their country. I was definitely told by the Dominican Ambassador to Cuba, Porfirio Rubirosa, that the government of the Dominican Republic was not aware of Batista's intention to seek asylum in Ciudad Trujillo. It was a case of "here I am."

Shortly after Batista's departure in the early morning hours of January 1, 1959, I received a telephone call from General Eulogio Cantillo confirming the departure of the President and advising me that he had been chosen by Batista to head the armed forces.

General Cantillo took over as Chief of Staff of the Army. Dr. Gustavo Pelayo was designated Premier. However, Fidel Castro refused to accept the appointment of Justice Piedra as

[2] I assisted these pilots in 1959 in removing their families from Cuba because their lives had been threatened by the Castro government.

provisional President, so the Supreme Court did not administer the oath of office to the Justice.

Fidel Castro immediately called a general strike on New Year's Day and demanded that Dr. Manuel Urrutia, former Judge of the Urgency Court of Santiago de Cuba be installed as the provisional President. The general strike was most effective. Hotels, cafés and grocery stores closed their doors. All forms of transportation were shut off.

For many hours, the people of Havana thought Batista's flight was just another *bola* (rumor). They could not believe it.

Chapter XIX

The Mob Takes Over

CUBA WAS CAUGHT without warning in an unguarded moment. The news struck the people like a bolt from the blue.

When broadcasts from the radio and television stations repeated the news of the fall of the government, the people began to attach weight to the report of Batista's flight. Crowds poured out of the buildings, cars raced through the streets with their horns blasting. Every radio and television station appealed to the people to be calm and to assist in maintaining order and issued warnings that looters and vandals would be treated harshly.

It was not until the middle of the day that the crowds

began to gather in the streets of Havana. By that time, the troops of the Directório Revolucionário (student group) were patrolling the streets in jeeps and in commandeered automobiles. Under the circumstances, they maintained remarkable control.

There was looting and rioting. Parking meters were destroyed; shop and restaurant windows were smashed. In the residential districts the homes of high Cuban government officials were looted, including the homes of Pilar García, Chief of the National Police. The pent-up emotions of the people found an outlet through violent outbreaks but the feared blood bath did not develop.

With Batista gone and the revolutionaries in control, the general strike was completely effective. No waiters in any hotels or restaurants would serve a meal. Transportation was completely shut off.

General Cantillo informed me as late as 9:00 A.M. on the morning of January 1 that planes were still leaving Cuba and that there were no restrictions on evacuations of people who wanted to leave Cuba. All Cuban Air Force pilots were told by General Cantillo they could leave the country if they wished or stay in Cuba and take their chances on future consequences. Most of them remained. At a later date, forty-three Cuban Air Force pilots stood trial and were acquitted. Their acquittal infuriated Castro. Under his orders, a new court was formed, so that the same pilots who had been acquitted could be tried again. At the new trial, supervised by Fidel and Raúl Castro, they were convicted and were given sentences of up to thirty years imprisonment.

The Cuban Ambassador to Washington, Nicolas Arroyo, resigned on the afternoon of January 1, shortly after Castro sympathizers gained admission to the Cuban Embassy in Washington. Dr. Emilio Pando, the Embassy's economic counselor, was left in charge.

Political prisoners were immediately freed in Havana and in the interior. The Cuban exiles in Florida were besieging Pan American and Cubana Airlines for space to return to Cuba. The Embassy had long before made its plans to take care of all eventualities. We were prepared to protect American citizens during the anticipated period of chaos. Consul General Brown was responsible for drawing up the Emergency Evacuation Plan. Daniel E. Braddock, Minister Counselor, was in charge of carrying out the plan.

Our first responsibility was to evacuate more than 2,000 American tourists and school children who were stranded in Cuba. Ships arriving in Havana were unable to dock owing to the strike. The United States Embassy immediately set about arranging transportation for all American students and tourists who asked for assistance.

My friend Daniel Taylor, president of the West Indies Fruit and Steamship Company, in response to a telephone call, arranged for a ship to come from Key West on January 3 to pick up stranded American, British and Canadian citizens. It was the policy of the Embassy to extend the same courtesies and privileges to British and Canadian citizens as to American citizens.

In Havana three car pools were established—each pool consisting of eighteen automobiles—to transport Americans from various centers in Havana to the airport and to the docks. The cars were loaned to the pool by officers of the Embassy and by American businessmen. Under the guidance of Minister Counselor Daniel Braddock and Eugene A. Gilmore, Chief of Economic Division, the officers of the Embassy did a splendid job in the evacuation proceedings.

Planes were leaving Cuba empty and returning from the United States with Cuban exiles. The situation had to be corrected. I asked the State Department not to let any more

Cubans leave the United States until the Castro officials permitted Americans to board outgoing Pan American planes.

More than 500 American tourists stranded in Cuba and running out of money were taken by sea, on the afternoon of January 3, to Key West, Florida, on board the car ferry, *City of Havana*, of the West Indies Fruit and Steamship Company. The same ship returned to Havana on January 4, after a seven-hour run, to pick up many hundreds more Americans who wanted to go home. Planes carried approximately 1,500 hungry, stranded Americans to Florida after the arrangements had been made.

The 26th of July Movement consented to Cubana Airlines evacuating Americans, but balked at the use of airlines belonging to American companies. I tried to get word through to Fidel Castro or to Raúl Castro to give us permission to use American planes. Pan American had six commercial airliners ready in Miami on a standby basis. However, the Castro people would not agree to the use of American planes.

American flags and stickers bearing the American emblem were displayed on all cars. There were barricades and men with guns every few blocks. When we drove up to a road block, our cars were allowed to pass through as soon as they recognized the people were Americans.

The Embassy issued the following press release on January 3:

The American Ambassador announced that at 2:00 A.M. today arrangements were completed whereby the 26th of July Movement agreed to allow Cubana Airlines to return American tourists and American students to the United States.

The 26th of July Movement agreed to a central assembly point and provided escorts for convoys to the airport. Three American Embassy convoys consisting of Embassy cars supplemented by private American resident cars started transferring passengers to the airport at 7:30 A.M. and will continue throughout the day.

All flights but one are shuttle flights to Miami. The other flight, carrying 90 Americans, left for New York City at 11:30 A.M.

In addition to available air flights, the SS *City of Havana*, an air conditioned car ferry, will return to Havana tonight, January 3, and will transport more American tourists to Key West the morning of January 4.

The operation is proceeding without incident, and the American Embassy is hopeful that all American tourists and American students will be returned to the United States today or tomorrow. 508 left last night and we hope to arrange for the departure of more than 400 today.

Due to the general strike, the 26th of July Movement has not permitted the Embassy to use other carriers.

The following paid advertisement, issued by the American Chamber of Commerce of Cuba, appeared in the *Havana Post* on January 6:

In order to avoid the possibility of an erroneous impression of the situation in Cuba, the American Chamber of Commerce of Cuba is interested in noting that to its knowledge none of the thousands of American residents has left Cuba on account of recent developments.

The hundreds who have left since the first of January were composed solely, in so far as we can learn, of tourists, transient business visitors and students returning from their vacations to classrooms in the United States. This was facilitated efficiently and courteously by the entire staff of the United States Embassy here for whom we have the warmest praise and made possible through the instant and ready co-operation of the Cuban authorities to whom goes our great appreciation.

An editorial appearing in the *Havana Post* stated that there had been much favorable comment regarding the manner in which the staff of the United States Embassy conducted themselves during the violent events in early January 1959. More than 2,000 Americans were evacuated by the American

Embassy to the United States on the first few days of the new regime. The *Havana Post* went on to say that this reflected great credit to the Embassy.

The following congratulatory, unclassified telegram was received on January 7 from Secretary of State John Foster Dulles:

To the Ambassador: Please accept my congratulations and those of the entire Department to you and all of your staff, for superior performance in carrying out the evacuation of American tourists from Cuba without injury to any persons and without any untoward incident. This was a fine demonstration of skill and teamwork and we are grateful for the excellent manner in which the operation was carried out. (Signed) Dulles.

As is always the case, there were some tourists who complained. I can remember several who could not understand why they had to carry their own bags when boarding the S.S. *City of Havana.*

On January 4 I received a message from William Wieland, Chief of the Caribbean Division, asking that I come to Washington immediately to discuss the recognition of Castro by the United States government, because the State Department wanted to recognize the Fidel Castro government as soon as possible. I said that I could not leave Cuba while we were evacuating Americans. It would be most unseemly for the American Ambassador to use a seat on a commercial airliner leaving Cuba when there were still American tourists to be evacuated. I said I would come to Washington as soon as the last American was safely evacuated.

On January 3, 1959, the Diplomatic Corps held a meeting at the residence of the Papal Nuncio, Monsignor Luis Centoz. The purpose of the meeting was to select a committee to inquire as to whether General Cantillo would honor the rights of asylum and give protection to the various Latin American Embassies. A committee was chosen composed of the Ambassadors to Cuba from Spain, Argentina, Chile, Brazil, the Papal Nuncio and myself.

The committee immediately proceeded to the Presidential Palace for an interview with General Cantillo, who assured us that protection would be given to the various Embassies and that the treaties between Latin American nations regarding the rights of asylum would be honored.

On the way out, I met Herbert Matthews on the steps of the Presidential Palace. He inquired as to the purpose of my visit to the palace. I told him the facts. Evidently he did not believe me because shortly thereafter I was called to the teletype in the Embassy by the State Department. William Wieland was at the Washington end, accompanied by William Snow, Deputy Assistant Secretary for Latin American affairs. Mr. Wieland inferred that I had been to the Presidential Palace with the purpose of backing a military junta to keep Fidel Castro from assuming power. He admitted the source of his information was Herbert Matthews, and asked if this was true. Whether Herbert Matthews reported to William Wieland to verify the purpose of my visit to the Presidential Palace, or whether his purpose was to make sure that nothing was to be done by the United States to interfere with his friend, Fidel Castro, taking over the government of Cuba I do not know. However, it was another indication of the close association between Herbert Matthews and the Fourth Floor of the State Department.

On January 5, 1959, I was at the airfield in Havana on my way to Washington when I received a phone call from Minister Counselor Daniel E. Braddock. He reported that there was tension in the air, and that fighting might break out in Havana. The Directório Revolucionário (rebel students) who still occupied the Presidential Palace, had not as yet agreed to turn the headquarters over to the 26th of July Movement. Upstairs in the Presidential Palace in Batista's ornate office,

Rolando Cubela, the youthful chief of the student group, was occupying Batista's chair; and there was some question as to whether the rebel group would turn over the Presidential Palace to Dr. Manuel Urrutia, Fidel Castro's designee as President of the new provisional government.

There was tense excitement at the airfield, due to the anticipated arrival of President Manuel Urrutia. Then word spread at the airfield that Dr. Urrutia would not land. His plane was heading back to Florida.

I cancelled my plans to leave and returned to the Embassy. However, fighting was averted when representatives of both factions negotiated evacuation of the Palace, permitting Dr. Urrutia's entry that evening.

So on January 6, 1959, accompanied by my wife, I left for Washington and landed at the Miami International airport in a United States military plane, piloted by my air attaché, Colonel E. S. Nichols. Rumors were rapidly spreading that soon I would be recalled. The *Miami News* on January 6 stated that they had learned that top officials of the provisional government of President Manuel Urrutia y Lleo had drafted papers for delivery to the United States State Department asking for the removal of Ambassador Smith as soon as possible.

The *Miami News* also said: "Smith has been a thorn for the Revolutionaries for several months. They repeatedly have charged that he was 'Neutral in favor of Batista the Dictator.'"

Castro's general counsel in the United States, Constantine Kangles, urged my immediate recall in a letter to Secretary of State Dulles. He charged: "Openly showing his (Smith's) hostility to Dr. Fidel Castro, the national hero of the Cuban people." And among other charges he wrote: "He has refused to even shake the friendly, extended hand of the Democratic leader (Castro)." I made no comment on the reports.

As soon as I reached Washington I went to Assistant

Secretary Roy Rubottom's office and was greeted with the words, "How do you stand with the new government under President Manuel Urrutia y Lleo?" I told him that he knew what my position was on the Castros.

Without more ado he asked me to accompany him to the fifth floor for an appointment with the Under Secretary, Christian Herter. I was informed by Secretary Herter that the United States government wanted to recognize the new government under President Urrutia immediately, and it had been decided that I should be recalled.

My instructions were to return to Havana that night or at the latest the next morning immediately to make an appointment with the new foreign minister, Roberto Daniel Agramonte, and deliver the United States note of recognition to the Cuban Foreign Ministry.

At the end of our conference Secretary Herter asked me to remain. After the others left, he said he had been instructed by President Eisenhower to offer me another Ambassadorial post. I expressed my appreciation and answered in the negative. This was a natural reaction at the time.

On January 7, my wife and I flew back to Havana after my hurried consultation at the State Department and I immediately made an appointment to deliver the note of recognition to the Foreign Minister, Agramonte. The State Department held an open telephone line with the Embassy, so that they could at once release the news. The recognition came six days after former President Fulgéncio Batista fled to the Dominican Republic.

Fidel Castro did not arrive in Havana until the next day, January 8, after making his way westward from the Provinces, making sure of municipal regimes behind him.

The United States usually withholds recognition from a new government until it is formally established and operating. Normally, the United States does not want to be among the first or among the last to recognize a new government. The United States usually waits until assurances are given that the new government will honor its international obligations. It was the custom for the United States to wait until several Latin American countries had recognized the new government. I testified before the Sub-Committee of the United States Senate:

"It has always been the policy of the United States not to be one of the first or one of the last to recognize a friendly government. It has always been the policy of the United States government, before they recognized a new government, to be sure of the following. I do not place them in order of their importance, but they are—(a) If a government is Communist or too much infiltrated with Communism. (b) Whether a government will honor its international obligations. (c) That the new government can maintain law and order. And we always hope that they have the support of the people. In this case, I believe that we were very hasty in the recognition of the Castro government."

According to an article in the *New York Times* of January 7, State Department officials said that the United States had been reassured about the stability and direction of the new government because the Cabinet represented a broad spectrum of anti-Batista Cubans. Several of the Cuban members, State Department officials said, were men of stature in their professions.

Neither I nor any official in the American Embassy had any conversation with a member of the new provisional government in Cuba regarding their intentions to honor their international obligations.

If we had taken the normal and usual precautions and adopted the normal procedures to receive assurances from Fidel Castro, before our recognition, that he would honor the international obligations of Cuba, we would have been in a stronger position in protecting the interests of American citizens. Fidel Castro unlawfully expropriated approximately one billion dollars of American investments. In addition, the United States government had invested $100,000,000 in the Nicaro Nickel property. No attempt at any compensation by the Cubans has ever been initiated.

It has always been the policy of the United States to recognize the inalienable rights of a foreign government to nationalize its own properties and its own land. However, in the past the United States insisted that American citizens receive equitable compensation for the property or investments which were to be expropriated. This was not done in Cuba.

The following is the note which I personally handed to Foreign Minister Roberto Daniel Agramonte:

I have been instructed by my Government to inform Your Excellency that having noted with satisfaction the assurances given by the new Government of Cuba of its intention to comply with the international obligations and agreements of Cuba, the Government of the United States is pleased to recognize the Government under the Presidency of Manuel Urrutia y Lleo as provisional government of the Republic of Cuba. At the same time the government of the United States expresses the sincere good will of the government and the people of the United States toward the new government and people of Cuba.

In the official note of recognition, the usual diplomatic language regarding assurances of international obligations was used. Yet Fidel Castro was not approached. Castro's government received official United States recognition before he arrived in Havana after making his triumphant progress across Cuba. Castro's designee for President, Manuel Urrutia, did not return to Cuba until the evening of January 5. On January 6 the Embassy received an official note advising us of the formation of the new Government of Cuba under the Presi-

dency of Dr. Manuel Urrutia y Lleo. On January 7, I personally delivered the official United States note of recognition.

I never talked to Fidel Castro. It was my intention to ask
for an appointment through the Foreign Ministry shortly after
his arrival in Havana. Any such thoughts on my part were
quickly dispelled after his public statement to a group of reporters in the lobby of the Havana Hilton Hotel. Castro's off-
hand remarks were that if the United States intervened to
protect its investments there would be 200,000 dead *gringos*
in the streets. After such belligerent and disrespectful remarks
about the United States, it was obvious that an interview between Fidel Castro and myself could serve no useful purpose.

Chapter XX

Castro Takes Over

WELL DO I REMEMBER the night, shortly after the bearded forces occupied Camp Columbia in early January 1959, when I saved a Cuban Army General's life.

Batista left General Eulogio Cantillo in command of the armed forces when he fled Cuba, with instructions to form a provisional government to govern Cuba until general elections could be held. When I last talked to General Cantillo, he told me that he was left in charge of a dead army. He was shortly replaced, on orders of Fidel Castro, by Colonel Ramón Barquin, who had been in prison on the Isle of Pines.

Colonel Barquin was in charge of the armed forces and

in command of Camp Columbia at the time of the arrival in Havana of the bearded army under the command of Commandante Cienfuegos. Colonel Barquin opened the gates of Camp Columbia and welcomed the revolutionary army. Cienfuegos and the bearded troops had arrived in Havana to hold fast the city while Fidel Castro was still making his way to the capital from the eastern end of the island. Che Guevara and his troops had taken command of the fortress at La Cabaña.

On the night of January 4, I learned from my senior military attaché, Air Force Colonel Nichols, that Mrs. Cantillo had received word that her husband, the General, was to face a firing squad early the next morning, on orders of Fidel Castro, because General Cantillo had permitted Batista to escape. Colonel Nichols asked if there was not something I could do to save the General's life. Through the American military attaché, Colonel Samuel Kail, an appointment was made with Major Camillo Cienfuegos for 2 A.M. at the military headquarters.

I telephoned the Brazilian Ambassador to Cuba, Vasco da Cunha, and asked if he would accompany me to Camp Columbia on my mission of compassion. I was relieved when Ambassador da Cunha agreed to accompany me, because I was acting as an individual on this mission and not in an official capacity; and I wanted a witness. Also the Ambassador was well known for his sympathy toward the motives of the revolutionaries.

In the early hours of the morning, I drove to the Ambassador's suburban residence in the Vedado district. There was shooting in the streets. The members of the Directório Revolucionário were fighting with the 26th of July forces. Vandals were still sacking and looting the homes of the Batista sympathizers. The city was in darkness. It reminded me of the blackout days in London during World War II.

The city was still under the control of the Directório Revolucionário forces. Fidel Castro's troops were held within the confines of the military headquarters.

When I arrived at the Brazilian Embassy the Youth Militia were firing on the residence of the Brazilian Ambassador. An armed 26th of July supporter accompanied the Ambassador from the Embassy and climbed in the front seat of the car. The distance from the Brazilian Embassy to Camp Columbia was approximately five miles. Although we had American flags flying from the fenders of the automobile, we were challenged every few blocks by civilian militia men.

Upon entering Camp Columbia, I was amazed to find the officers of the Cuban Army mingling on a fraternal basis with the bearded officers. While we waited for our audience with Cienfuegos, Ambassador da Cunha introduced me to a stout, friendly bearded man who, he said, had sought asylum in the Brazilian Embassy. I learned from the Ambassador that this individual had been the second in command of Batista's Military Intelligence for approximately two years. All that time he had been one of Castro's most valuable spies.

After some delay, we were shown into a small room where I saw Major Cienfuegos for the first time. He was formerly a Cuban baseball player and a dishwasher in New York. The group reminded me of pictures I had seen of the Dillinger gang. They were dirty, unshaven, shoeless, and well armed.

Cienfuegos had a pleasing personality. He was courteous but aloof and informed us that only Fidel Castro could cancel the orders for the impending execution of General Cantillo.

I told him that if General Cantillo was executed without a fair trial or even a hearing the 26th of July Movement would lose face in world opinion. I reasoned with Cienfuegos that it was in the best interest of Fidel Castro and the revolutionary movement to delay the order for the General's execution. Ambassador da Cunha supported my position. Cienfuegos agreed, but could not rescind the order without the approval of Castro. He finally agreed to a delay of the execution and said he would inform Castro immediately of our conversation.

As soon as I left Camp Columbia, I reported our conversation to Mrs. Cantillo. The General was not executed, and the next day I had a long and heartwarming talk with Mrs. Cantillo. She asked if I would obtain asylum for her, which I obtained in a small Latin American Embassy. However, she later changed her mind, saying that she wished to remain by her husband's side.

That night, for over two hours, Fidel Castro raved and ranted over the television against General Cantillo because he had permitted Batista to leave the island. Castro said the General would have a trial but that he personally would be responsible for seeing that the General was convicted. At a later date, General Eulogio Cantillo was tried, convicted, and sentenced to fifteen years imprisonment on the Isle of Pines.

Cienfuegos was not unreasonable. He had agreed to our request to postpone the execution of General Cantillo. Later, due to unexplainable circumstances, the airplane which bore Cienfuegos from Camaguey to Havana disappeared. Up to the time that I left Cuba, there was no trace or clue as to the whereabouts of the plane, the pilot or Cienfuegos. This was difficult to understand because the flight between the two cities is over normal terrain all the way. The rumor was that Castro had ordered his death. Cienfuegos was admired and respected by the rebels. Because of his beard and young face Cubans referred to him as "El Cristo." He was not the type to follow Castro's orders blindly, and it was believed that he was unsympathetic to the Communist control of the 26th of July Movement.

As experience has proven time and again, United States interests are best served by changing Ambassadors following governmental upheaval as explosive as that which had just occurred in Cuba. On January 10, 1959, I officially resigned as the United States Ambassador. My letter of resignation to the President follows:

In the period of time from 1957 to 1959, during which I have had the honor of serving as your Ambassador to Cuba, I have been fortunate enough to have had a part in one of the great historical Latin-American dramas of our century. I have watched Cuba strike through a political cocoon to what we all hope will be freedom.

Following a governmental upheaval as explosive as that which has just occurred in Cuba, I sincerely believe it is in the best interests of the United States to change its Ambassador. Therefore, I respectfully ask that you accept my resignation as your Ambassador to Cuba.

I shall take this opportunity to return to private life and to my long-neglected business affairs.

I then received the following reply from President Eisenhower:

Dear Mr. Ambassador:

It is with deep appreciation of your service to the nation as Ambassador to Cuba since July 1957 that I regretfully accept your resignation from that post. You have served there with dignity and dedication in an epoch of Cuban history which placed unusually difficult demands on you. You have responded to these demands with distinguished performance and I am grateful to you for the services you have rendered. The government and people of this country have long watched with you the unfolding developments in Cuba. We all earnestly hope as you do that the people of that friendly country so close to us in geography and sentiment will through freedom find peace, stability and progress. I wish you and your family every happiness on the resumption of your personal affairs which you have so long neglected in order to serve your country. With warm personal regards.

Sincerely yours, *Dwight D. Eisenhower.*

One year before Batista fled Cuba, on January 16, 1958, I went on record at a press conference held at the State Department that I did not believe Fidel Castro's government would ever honor its international obligations, that I did not believe that Fidel Castro could maintain law and order, and that I was sure that it would not be in the best interests of Cuba or the United States for him to assume power. From that time on the Communists and the Fidel Castro sympathizers did everything to discredit me and impair my effectiveness.

The day after my resignation (January 11, 1959) *Bohemia* magazine published a scurrilous attack accusing me of being a "servant of the Despot." For months this magazine had been under strict government censorship, as its publisher, Miguel Angel Quevedo, was violently pro-Castro and anti-Batista. Now he was free to spew out his pent-up hates. Quevedo is an example of those publishers who were unwitting tools of the Communist propaganda apparatus.

This is the beginning of the article from *Bohemia* magazine, as translated from Spanish at the Havana Embassy:

From this office of the Ambassador of the United States, Earl E. T. Smith, after a door banged, a strong man with a firm step and the air of a professor came out. His face was blushed with ire. He was so troubled that he seemed to be deaf to the excuses made by the diplomats who followed him. The incident could not be dissipated by merely a few high sounding words.

Very few were acquainted with the angry vision in the refrigerated environment of the fifth floor but very soon his name passed from mouth to mouth: Homer Bigart of the *New York Times*.

A few minutes later the incident at the American diplomatic headquarters went beyond its walls and became the subject of discussion over highball glasses at the National Hotel. Mr. Bigart himself told his colleagues who had come from the United States to cover the Cuban situation: "I went to see the Ambassador to inquire into his reaction when he was informed of my sudden departure from Havana to go to the Sierra Maestra." Again the round face of the veteran newsman honored with two Pulitzer prizes became red in telling of his talk with Smith: "How is it possible," asked the Ambassador, "that you have gone to the Sierra Maestra to talk to those Communists?"

"Those people are not Communists, Mr. Ambassador."

"Don't tell me that. Fidel Castro is a Communist with a small band of criminals who are engaged in killing and stealing in the mountains of Oriente."

After repeating the dialogue, Bigart, with his blond hair over his forehead looked on the faces of his colleagues to get a reaction from them, and harsh expressions soon came forth.

Still indignant, Bigart wrote in the *New York Times* on Sunday, March 23, 1958, "If the present policy continues with regard to Cuba the United States will be left with but a single friend: Dictator Fulgéncio Batista."

The article in *Bohemia* magazine went on to accuse me of having sold out to Batista and to the Freeport Sulphur Company. According to Mr. Quevedo, Batista had purchased my support for his government by granting favorable tax concessions to the Moa Bay Mining Company, subsidiary of the Freeport Sulphur Company. The article further implied that I had been bought by the Freeport Sulphur Company to obtain for the company a favorable grant of tax exemption from the Batista government. The facts were that the terms of the agreement between the Freeport Sulphur Company and the government of Cuba had been approved by both parties before my arrival in Cuba.

I had the complete article sent over the teletype to Assistant Secretary Roy Rubottom and asked for an official denial. I further said, in substance:

I do not care what this magazine says, but I cannot ignore any reflections upon my honesty. There are two things I will not be called—one is a crook, the other is a fairy.

On January 15, 1959, the State Department, through the United States Embassy in Cuba, issued the following release:

Castro Takes Over

In response to inquiries, the American Embassy announces that neither the State Department nor the American Embassy ever intervened during the negotiations of the new industry concessions granted by the Cuban Government to Moa Bay Mining Company in August 1957. Negotiations were completed in July 1957, before Ambassador Smith's arrival in Cuba, and the subsequent decree granting the concessions was published in August 1957. The only interest which the United States Government showed in the project here was to express, at an earlier date, its general interest in the Moa Bay project, because this project would provide nickel and cobalt—metals of interest to the United States for whose purchase the United States government had already signed a contract with the Freeport Sulphur Company, parent company of Moa Bay.

Chapter XXI

Duties and Technique of an Ambassador

THE CERTIFICATE OF APPOINTMENT from the President of the United States to an Ambassador reads:

Reposing special trust and confidence in your Integrity, Prudence, and Ability, I have nominated and by and with the advice and consent of the Senate do appoint you Ambassador Extraordinary and Plenipotentiary of the United States of America to —————, authorizing you hereby to do and perform all such matters and things as to the said place of Office do appertain, or as may be duly given you in charge hereafter, and the said office to hold and exercise during the pleasure of the President of the United States for the time being.

Duties and Technique of an Ambassador

The Ambassador is the personal representative of the President of the United States. It is the duty of the Ambassador to develop a close understanding not only with the government, but also with the people of the country to which he is assigned. He should convey a sympathetic and accurate understanding of America, and create friends for the United States. The Embassy must have a close understanding of the people, their cultures and their institutions.

It is the duty of the Ambassador to oversee and co-ordinate all the activities of the United States in the country to which he is accredited. The Ambassador is in charge of the entire United States diplomatic mission and should supervise all its operations. The mission includes—in addition to the personnel of the State Department and the Foreign Service—also the representatives of all other United States agencies which have activities in the country.[1]

The representatives of other agencies are expected to communicate directly with their own offices in Washington, yet they are instructed to look to the Ambassador for guidance and to keep him fully informed.

Today, because of modern communications, decisions of an Ambassador are limited to those made on the spot and emergency ones. An Ambassador represents his country and speaks for his country, but all policy decisions are made in the Department of State. It is the duty of an Ambassador to keep the Department fully informed at all times. In the Havana Embassy we had approximately 300 men and women serving under the Chief of Mission. This number included service attachés and Military Assistance Advisory Groups. The Embassy collected, evaluated, and transmitted all local information. The over-all collection, collation, evaluation, and dissemination of information is done in Washington.

The Deputy Under Secretary of State for Administration,

[1] Foreign Affairs Manuel, Vol. 2, Jan. 16, 1962, 020. 1 (p. 1).

Mr. Loy Henderson, had his problems in obtaining the resignation of some Ambassadors at the end of President Eisenhower's first term. It is the standard and accepted procedure for Ambassadors, Cabinet members, and all Presidential appointees to tender their resignation to the President before the completion of his term of office. The President, if re-elected for a second term, is then free to make whatever new appointments he chooses, without any stigma being attached to the incumbents.

This prompted the Deputy-Secretary to make it clear to me, and, I assume to others, that my appointment would terminate at the conclusion of President Eisenhower's second term, and that I should not have any false hopes of becoming a perennial Ambassador. I assured the Under Secretary that he need have no fears as to my ambitions along these lines.

All cables from an Embassy to the State Department are automatically addressed to the Secretary of State. When received in the State Department, they are routed according to departmental procedure. An Ambassador has the privilege to direct a cable personally to anyone up to and including the President. When there was a matter of importance, I would address my messages to Assistant Secretary Rubottom directly. I did not feel it was correct to go over his head. I do not believe an Ambassador should be the judge of what goes over the head of the Assistant Secretary of State, especially when there are so many, day-by-day, important decisions to be made affecting our relations with a politically turbulent country, such as Cuba was.

Among free men, every man has a right to an opinion, and to express it. The newspaper reporters expressed their opinions daily. Yet some of these reporters lacked a sense of responsibility. An Ambassador is hampered by the many self-appointed ambassadors, such as the press corps, who, for example, descend upon Cuba to write a good story. As a result of the opinions expressed by the liberal ones, Cubans acquired the impression that they could obtain results through pressuring the press and playing upon the sympathetic reactions of those who instinctively side with the underdog. Fidel Castro himself was a good example of appreciating the power of the press and being fully aware of the necessity for good public relations. He was always available to reporters.

For many years the subject of career men versus political appointees has been continuous. The phrase political appointee is misleading. What is meant is that the President selects a person of proven abilities who has been successful in his particular field. Such men have had much experience and can often be more effective than career men in particular situations. Out of a population of nearly 185,000,000 persons much talent exists and much can be used. The assumption that career men should have a monopoly on ambassadorial appointments to foreign embassies is illogical. On both sides there have been many distinguished men and many incompetent men.

In my opinion, the most essential qualification in an Ambassador, is good judgment and the courage to act on that judgment. A career officer with equally good judgment is intimidated by his awareness that in service life—whether it be in the armed services or in the foreign service—it is more advantageous for continuing advancement to maintain on vital issues an acceptable attitude rather than one based on personal convictions.

The Ambassador has the authority to send back to the United States any individual members of the Mission who are not, in the Ambassador's judgment, functioning effectively—reporting the circumstances to the Department of State.[2]

It is customary to hold daily staff meetings. Every morning, I would hold a staff meeting in my office, attended by the Deputy Chief of Mission, the Consul General, the Counselor

[2] Foreign Affairs Manual, Vol. 2—020, 1 (p. 1), 1-16-62.

for Economic Affairs, the First Secretary for Political Affairs, Armed Forces Attachés, Press Attaché, the Public Affairs Officer, Chief, United States Operations Mission to Cuba (Point Four), and the Legal and Political Attachés.

Once a month, we would have a meeting of the country team, which included all of the above, plus the Agricultural Attaché; the Labor Attaché; the Members of the Military Assistance Advisory Groups; and those serving with other Military components attached to the Mission.

Shortly after an Ambassador presents his credentials to the Chief of State he must make formal calls on each and every Ambassador, and these Ambassadors make formal calls in return. Ambassadors' wives are expected to follow the same procedure.

My wife and I gave receptions of 250-400 persons for visiting dignitaries, Congressmen, Chambers of Commerce, Boards of Trade, newspaper people, etc. In addition, we entertained, in 1957, the American business community, the Diplomatic Corps, Cuban press, Cuban society, Cuban politicians, Cuban labor leaders, and the Cuban clergy. Also, we made it a point to see that every individual attached to the American Embassy (Cubans and Americans) was invited to at least one reception at the Embassy Residence.

I was allowed an annual expenditure of approximately $7,000 for entertainment. If the Ambassador wants to do an adequate job of representation he has to spend much more than that—many times more in some Embassies. An Ambassador must be able to entertain at his own expense, which often means that he actually serves without compensation.

After the spring of 1958 we curtailed our entertaining, as we did not feel it was proper to give large receptions in view of the political unrest in the country.

The American Embassy is expected to be represented at functions of American business groups. Either I or the Deputy

Chief of Mission attended such affairs. The Ambassador should take active part in the Community Chest; speak at various functions; speak at the American Club on American holidays; hold receptions on July 4th; attend church services and speak before all church denominations; pay tribute to the memory of American war dead on Memorial Day.

My wife instituted the Florence Pritchett Smith Scholarship for Commercial Design enabling Cubans to study in the United States in the fields of commercial design. This was the number one project in which my wife was interested during her stay in Cuba. A great believer in the value of foreign exchange student programs, Florence's premise in establishing this particular program was to help the creative, artistic people of Cuba. She had spent many hours wandering through little shops, markets and artists' studios, observing the beautiful work done by Cubans in wood, marble and many other native products. Having spent years in and around the New York world of fashion, she was well aware of the native ability but also cognizant of the lack of professional or tasteful presentation of their products. She felt if American know-how in commercial design could be applied to native products, the exchange would benefit everyone, and, therefore, help create good will between our two countries.

After several meetings, a board of leading Cuban bankers, educators, and intellectuals was formed with Dr. José Ignacio de la Camara, vice-president of the Trust Company of Cuba as President of the Scholarship. There were also several board members of the Instituto Cultural Norte Americano on the board, for the scholarship was under the aegis of that institute. Francis Donahue, the Cultural Attaché of the Embassy, was an able and willing assistant to my wife during these difficult, long months of planning. He had much experience in the field of student scholarships and his advice was appreciated by both of us.

After a trip to New York Florence enlisted the ready support of six outstanding American leaders in the world of business and fashion. She returned home very gratified by the extraordinary enthusiasm shown in the scholarship by Americans. Everyone was willing to help. The American board consisted of Melvin Dawley, president of Lord and Taylor; Andrew Goodman, president of Bergdorf Goodman; Adam Gimbel, president of Saks Fifth Avenue; Vincent Draddy, president of David Crystal; Raymond Loewey, the internationally known industrial designer; and Maurice Newton of Hallgarten and Co. The Institute of International Education agreed to administer the scholarship, once the funds were raised.

On the belief that a venture shared jointly is better than a gift, the Cuban board raised their own contributions and the American fund raising was achieved through a ball given by the American Ball Committee at the Waldorf-Astoria on November 21, 1958. It was called a "Cuban Gala Night," and many of Florence's friends in New York served on the committee and made it a great success. The Cuban committee arranged for first-rate Cuban music and entertainment to be flown to New York by Cubana Airlines so the American audience could hear some of the beautiful, authentic music which is such an outstanding part of Cuban culture. Florence always said her committee was the prettiest fund raising committee in New York. Evidently they were, for *Life* photographed them in color and put them on the cover.

The winner of this three-year scholarship would attend an American school of design for one year with all expenses paid. The second year he would be employed by a firm specializing in his particular field of design. The third year he would return to Cuba and be assisted in starting in business. The first winner of the competitions held in Havana was a sensitive, talented young man who wanted to become a dress designer. He showed great promise during his work at the Parsons School of Design, so much so that the board of the scholarship program was considering giving him an extra year of study at Parsons. Unfortunately, the stress of living in America while his mother was in Cuba where conditions were politically disturbed became too much for him and he left school and returned home. The winner of the second competition was a bright, industrious young woman who refused the prize she had sought because she wanted to get married. Then Fidel Castro took over Cuba and the scholarship had to be abandoned until a future date. Florence had spent well over a year of hard work setting up this program, and it was indeed frustrating to have started something and because of political upheavals to find such odds against its successful continuance.

Being interested in baseball I awarded a trophy to the player selected by the experts as the most distinguished competitor in the current Cuban league baseball season. I also inaugurated contests for "The Responsible Citizenship Award."

In May 1958 we were celebrating in the United States the Centennial of Theodore Roosevelt's birth. The underlying element of this centennial was a rededication of the American people to the theme of responsible citizenship, a theme so well exemplified by Theodore Roosevelt, not only in words but also by his actions.

In an address delivered to the high school graduating class of the William T. Sampson School at Guantánamo Bay, I announced a new program for American high school students in Cuba, designed to reward them for having maintained high standards of personal conduct, leadership, tolerance, co-operation, and service. I said that American students could emulate Theodore Roosevelt by developing his high sense of responsibility as an individual American citizen. "You, as well as I,"

I continued, "represent and symbolize the United States to people here in Cuba. How you act and what you do is considered typical of Americans of your age group."

The program consisted of two awards given that year to responsible American citizens, students in the last four years of their secondary school career, who best exemplified the principles of American citizenship, put into practice in Cuba during their present academic year.

The two winners of the Responsible Junior American Citizenship awards were given an all-expense tour to Washington, D.C., to participate in one of the Theodore Roosevelt Centennial programs. The Theodore Roosevelt Association and I were co-sponsors for the trips.

Recipients of the awards were selected on the basis of recommendations from their schools concerning their records as representative American citizens abroad and also on the basis of a competitive essay examination.

It was my intention, upon arrival in Cuba, to observe a line of demarcation between cordial diplomatic correctness and personal friendship toward Batista. I followed this policy faithfully at all times and often it was difficult to adhere to this policy. President and Mrs. Batista had a son the same age as our son Earl. They were devoted parents and wanted their son to know an American boy. We frequently had to refuse invitations from President and Mrs. Batista for our boy to spend weekends with their son at their home at Veradero Beach or at their country place, Finca Kuquine. If our child were seen playing about the President's home it would immediately connote a close family-to-family relationship that did not exist.

Even buying a dog for your son had implications. My wife flew to Palm Beach in November to pick up a black poodle. There were three reporters and two photographers on hand at the Palm Beach International Airport. "Is this the dog you

(216)

and the Ambassador are giving Batista as a birthday present?" they asked. Such was the story that came out of Havana.

Five months had elapsed since our arrival in Cuba and we had not invited President Batista to the Residence of the American Embassy. There were still some people who were not aware of the fact that cordial relations had been renewed, since the Santiago incident, between the President and the American Ambassador. Florence and I knew that the time was now propitious to give a dinner for the President.

One point in our favor to explain the lapse in time, though it worked against us in every other respect, was the unlivable condition of the Embassy Residence. Our initial official entertaining had to be done in the National Hotel or in restaurants and all Cuba knew it. However, according to protocol certain entertaining should be completed within a reasonable time after the arrival of an Ambassador at a new post. The state dinner of a newly appointed American Ambassador for the President of Cuba has a time limit. Since everyone knew the Residence was being redone, the dates of formal receptions and state dinners were allowed to wait.

In late December 1957 a series of events occurred which clearly pointed to our need to give a dinner in honor of the President, regardless of whether the Residence was in condition or not. My wife invited two guests to dine with us and attend a dance at the Havana Country Club. The rumor was that Batista would be there. After dinner as we drove through the Country Club grounds, it was obvious this was true. Gun-toting guards were stationed everywhere. Friends living at the Club told us they were disturbed in the late afternoon by detectives who were making a thorough search and inspection. Some rooms had to be hastily vacated since they overlooked the dance floor on the terrace. The silent men with guns stood behind these louvered windows until the dancing stopped.

Our foursome joined a large, laughing, chatting group of

Cubans. Some time later my wife got up to dance. To reach the floor she had to walk through a narrow alley between two tables. In doing so she walked behind the President of the Republic. She was well aware of his presence as was everyone in the room. As she passed him, they both bowed pleasantly and she continued on. Immediately this created all sorts of chatter throughout the room. "She didn't speak." "He didn't speak." "What does that mean?" On it went as only rumors can spread in Cuba. The fact that my wife should not stop and address herself to the President to whom she had never been presented was not considered. The point that the President of the country did not rise and speak to her because they had not met was not considered. They both did what was correct for though they had not officially met, they bowed politely and she continued on.

The time was ripe for us to invite the President to the Embassy, so I asked Foreign Minister Guell to inform the President of our desire to give a state dinner in his honor and to please let us know what date would be convenient to the President.

Just before President Batista was to pay his first formal call on the Embassy—an event demanding a tremendous amount of planning on the part of my wife—we received news that Peter Van Ingen, my grandson, who was visiting us had come down with chicken pox. President Batista, when advised of this, phoned to say that fortunately all of his staff had already had chicken pox. So the party could go on as planned.

A list was submitted to us by the Foreign Minister of the Cabinet members who must be included. Then we submitted a list of the rest of the guests for the government's approval. It was my wife's feeling that since Batista had been to so many state dinners we should add a few young couples who were fun and attractive.

Other than the large state dining room, which was in order, the only other furnished room in the Embassy was the library, which was used for cocktails and after dinner, and was only large enough to seat fifteen comfortably. We had to plan the evening around the terraces of the Residence so we all prayed for a warm night. While my wife organized the seated dinner for fifty with a four-piece Cuban band after dinner, she also had to plan sandwiches and coffee for some thirty SIM (military intelligence men) who would patrol the grounds while the President was in the Residence of the American Embassy. United States security men went over the Residence and interviewed the extra servants hired for the night. A foreign Embassy cannot afford to take a chance when the President of the country visits the Embassy. We took no chances. A Cuban government helicopter circled the house while Batista was there.

Then came the bad news. That morning a freezing spell hit Cuba and the temperature fell to about 40 degrees. Florence learned it would be still colder that night. Now we found ourselves in the awkward position of giving a state dinner for fifty for the President of the Republic with only one comfortable room. This situation could prove to be most embarrassing.

This posed a problem. There were no caterers in Havana from whom to rent furniture and there was no way to heat the terraces. Florence was understandably upset. We knew if the party was not just right it would be the talk of the island next day. From such small circles large problems can grow. It was the Duke de Talleyrand, on leaving for the Vienna Conference, who, when queried by Louis XVIII about further instruction, replied, "Sire, I have more need of casseroles than I do of instructions." In the morning, as I left for the Chancellery, she said, "Don't worry, I am going to arrange this with a large American imagination and a small amount of equipment. As long as it is a good party no one will care."

After dinner, at the request of President Batista, Anita

Colby, who was our house guest, was seated next to the President because he was curious about career women. She regaled him with amusing tales of the trials of a career girl, and he was highly entertained.

At state dinners in Cuba, it is customary for the President to leave between 1:00 and 1:30 A.M. At 1:00 A.M., I noticed that President Batista was having a good time. A few minutes later I told Batista, "I will put away my watch if you will put away yours." The entire party, including the President, did not leave until 3:30 A.M.

It was a great party and the talk of Havana. The formula? Florence moved outside terrace furniture into the big empty salon and turned it into a night club. She used palms to fill empty corners; she covered glass-topped outside tables with pink clothes and gay bouquets of red and pink carnations as centerpieces. She transferred wall candelabras from other empty rooms to the salon, filled them with flickering red candles, and lit the fire in the fireplace. After the formality of dinner in the state dining room, where the table was festooned with assorted false fruits and Happiness roses (Marta Batista's favorite rose), it was unexpected to enter a gay, cozy little night club. About an hour later, again stressing the night club atmosphere, Florence spoke to everyone in Spanish over the mike and invited certain guests to entertain us. She had found out that the Prime Minister's wife loved to sing. Several wives of Cabinet members also had talent and she knew ahead of time that they would be ready and willing. Rather than a too formal state dinner, it was a festive, informal party at which much rapprochement was established.

On Christmas Day, 1957, my wife and I instituted the idea of holding a Christmas party at the American Embassy Residence for poor and needy children rather than a Christmas cocktail party for members of the American Colony. These children were victims of broken homes, some orphans and others living in institutions because their parents were unable to provide for them.

So that the group would be representative, my wife asked Francis Donahue to select ten different welfare organizations to invite ten children each, a total of 100. Three buses transported the children from the Chancellery out to the Residence, where approximately 100 American children of the Embassy group waited as their hosts. We thought the Cuban children would feel better if it appeared to be a party for Americans and Cubans.

In my wife's own words:

A tremendous lawn extending down to the pool had been gayly decorated with balloons, twinkling lights, candy canes, and wreaths. By a huge Christmas tree in the hall we waited to greet each child as he filed past, mute with excitement and anticipation. The children ranged from five to ten years in age and represented all religions and races.

After an hour of Mickey Mouse and other cartoons in the Embassy dining room, they were told to form a line and holding hands run double time to the outside lawn. While they ran down the lawn a helicopter (lent for the occasion by Minister of Public Works, Nicolas Arroyo) circled overhead, coming lower and lower. The children could hardly contain themselves when the copter landed on the lawn and out stepped a big, fat, heavily laden Santa Claus!

The reaction was universal. Cubans and Americans alike clustered around Santa calling, "Do you have a present for me, Santa?" and he did. He had a present for every child there with his name on it so each child knew and believed it was really for him. David Marx of the Marx Toy Company had generously contributed all the presents, and the Embassy wives had worked long and hard to wrap and label each one. The wives also helped decorate the lawn, for they were an enthusiastic group. Once the helicopter disappeared into the sunset hot dogs, ice cream, and cake were gobbled up by the children.

Then, as we wandered about the lawn, a set of still lifes was projected in front of our eyes, which stressed dramatically the need to begin with the children of the world if we want to achieve true international friendship. A small Cuban with chocolate ice cream running down his chin was head to head with a little American in deep concentration over how to work a wind-up plane, and two Cuban boys with big, sad eyes were holding their *perro caliente* (hot dog, in English) while a small American girl spread mustard on it. It was a scene of torn paper, candy-covered faces, and ice cream melting on both Spanish and American shirt fronts, and the mutual understanding and sharing of the moment was encouraging and gave you a feeling of hope for the future.

As twilight darkened into night, and Christmas lights were twinkling in all the Residence windows, the buses pulled away to the echo of sweet Spanish voices calling, "*Hasta luego, muchas gracias, Felices Pascuas.*"

At the customary United States Embassy staff Christmas party, held on December 23, 1957, we were privileged to hear a few words from the guest of honor, the incumbent United States Senator, John F. Kennedy of Massachusetts, who was visiting us at the Embassy. I introduced the Senator by saying, "We are all fortunate to be able to hear a few words from the Senator from Massachusetts, who may very well be our next President."

My experience with the Diplomatic Corps was gratifying and enlightening. Although the interests and influence of other nations in Cuba did not approach that of the United States, the understanding and sympathetic support to what I was trying to achieve was always helpful. They were cognizant of the responsibility of the people of the United States to the people of Cuba. In some cases the United States and other countries shared similar difficulties during periods. For example, Stanley Fordham, the Ambassador from Great Britain to Cuba, was under considerable criticism from the revolutionaries because of the sale of British fighter planes to the Batista government. The Spanish Ambassador, Juan Pablo Lojendio, was an intense and proud representative of a proud nation. There was in Cuba a large Spanish colony and many Spaniards held positions of importance in the Church. Ambassador Lojendio became so irate and disgusted at the television tirades of untruths delivered against Spain by Fidel Castro that he went on television to contradict the lies of Castro.

Months after my departure from Cuba, Ambassador Lojendio became furious after listening to another tirade. He drove to the television studio, burst in on Castro, interrupting him in the middle of his hysterical berating against Spain. He shook his finger in Castro's face and reprimanded him in front of the television audience. Castro notified the Spanish government that their Ambassador was persona non grata. Although undiplomatic, it was the natural reaction of a proud Spaniard defending the honor of his country against the malicious beratings of the former bandit now become statesman.

The Diplomatic Corps in Cuba during my stay were a thoughtful group who comported themselves with dignity. They hoped for a peaceful solution to Cuba's political problems. During our frequent exchange of views, I established many close friendships and I was touched by their sympathetic reaction when, on my departure from Cuba, they presented to me, in a group, a large silver cigarette box. The presentation was made at a special ceremony at the residence of the Papal Nuncio. On the top of the box was a map of the Island of Cuba, with six small sapphires indicating the major cities in each of the six provinces.

Chapter XXII

What Does It All Mean?

NO MATTER what coloration is put on it, the fact remains that international Communism has established a base ninety miles from our shores, from which it is organizing against the United States throughout Latin America.

It does not matter at all that we have allies close to the Russian border; what does matter is that the Russians had not established a base on the Western hemisphere until Castro appeared in Cuba.

From my experience in Cuba I have concluded that this need not have happened. That it did happen was, to a surprising degree, due to the policy of many in critical positions in the State Department that a Leftist dictator was better than a Rightist dictator, even though the Rightist dictator may be friendly to the United States and the Leftist dictator our enemy. The test with them is not what is beneficial to the United States but what fits their doctrinaire views of the future world.

It is very difficult to understand this policy from an American point of view. I found, as Ambassador to Cuba, that I could not understand this policy as it applied to Cuba. Granted that Batista had outlived his usefulness, the alternative certainly need not have been Castro, our enemy. And it must be noted that Castro would not have been in the position to attain power and could not have created the agency to seize power without the good will of the Fourth Floor.

It cannot be maintained that the government of the United States was unaware that Raúl Castro and Che Guevara, the top men of the 26th of July Movement are Communists, affiliated with international Communism. There was ample evidence to that effect. I have shown in this book that it was impossible for Assistant Secretary of State Roy Rubottom, his associate William Wieland, and the Fourth Floor not to be aware of Fidel Castro's Communist affiliations. It is beyond possibility that the CIA did not know. Roy Rubottom was in Bogotá when Fidel Castro, at the age of twenty-two, was an active organizer of Communist insurrection.

But I am sure that the Secretary of State and the Under-Secretary of State, and the President were not adequately and correctly informed on this subject, until it was too late. It is essential to understand this because while the Cuban situation may have to run its course, it ought not to be possible for the top officials of the United States to be kept in the dark on a matter of policy.

This then raises these questions:

What is really our policy? Who makes it? How is it established? Why did we intervene in Castro's favor in Cuba, when we might have supported able, knowledgeable pro-American men?

If dictatorship *versus* democracy were the only question that faced us, it would not be difficult to make a decision. However, as we are in the midst of a struggle for survival, other considerations are pertinent. Furthermore, to remove one dictator for another does not produce democracy.

If the policy of the United States is to bring about the overthrow of dictators in the hope that democracy will follow, then I believe that the United States must be prepared to take whatever steps are necessary to preserve law and order and prevent chaos during that interim period of transition which may last a long time. If free and open elections are to be held in these nations when a dictator is overthrown, a provisional government must be formed and such government needs outside support to maintain law and order. To do otherwise leaves a vacuum in which the Communists gain control. Such a vacuum did occur in Cuba. A group was ready to seize power, a Communist group, and we aided them to seize power.

We state that our policy is non-intervention, and through our actions imply that the Monroe Doctrine is dead. But we intervene positively or negatively or by innuendo every day. We intervene when we contract to sell armored cars or training planes or whatever, and then withhold what we have agreed to sell even after payment has been advanced. This is intervention to place the existing government in an embarrassing position, unable adequately to defend itself against bandit and Communist-supported forces. The psychological effect of the withdrawal of American support was devastating. That is negative intervention. We permit the Leftist dictator to establish a base for operations in the United States, in violation of our neutrality laws, and the State Department deals

(226)

with his emissaries. That is positive intervention. We influence other governments not to sell arms to the government of Cuba. That is intervention by innuendo.

If we are to intervene sufficiently to bring about the overthrow of dictatorships then we should intervene to whatever extent is required to fulfill our purpose. Otherwise, in my opinion, we must wait for the normal self-development of a people and not assist revolution of any kind. And we must be prepared to receive the criticism of supporting friendly governments recognized by the United States, although they have been labeled dictatorships.

To make my point clear, let me say that we helped to overthrow the Batista dictatorship, which was pro-American and anti-Communist, only to install the Castro dictatorship which was Communist and anti-American. Because democracy is successful in the United States, influential persons on the Fourth Floor believe that we must transplant and implant our ideas and our form of democracy to all other nations, many of whom are not yet prepared for, and are not suited to our form of government and do not like it. After all, a people has a right to its own form of government and its own way of life.

I testified to the Senate that I had learned from experience and observation that our policies are determined by influential individuals in the lower echelon of the State Department in their day-by-day actions. By the time the higher officials receive them policies have already been made and they have to live by them. In this book I have quoted from testimony of four other Ambassadors who testified under oath to the same effect. It comes too late to correct the errors of the desk-men, who often become so devoted to the countries to which they are assigned that they forget that their business is the United States. The Fourth Floor consists of desk-men, as they are called. They are career Foreign Service Officers who frequently look upon political appointees as here today and gone to-morrow.

After this book is published, some will wish to accuse me of attacking the entire Foreign Service. This is not my intent or my desire. I learned from experience to have a high regard and respect for many Foreign Service Officers.

While it is impossible to condemn an entire body of men, it is neither impossible nor incorrect to say that a structure of organization is such that men on a certain level on an organizational chart, lacking final political responsibility but having the power of day-by-day decision in political matters, can create a situation which may lead to national damage.

Many people will consider this as too sweeping an assertion. Yet this was true in the case of Cuba. The Secretary of State was preoccupied with Peking, Moscow, and Berlin. Policy decisions on Cuban affairs were determined on the Fourth Floor of the State Department, where influential persons believed in the revolution and hoped for its success. So far as I know, no definite policy governing our attitude to the friendly government of Cuba was set on the fifth floor (the top echelon of the State Department).

The Secretary of State did not, during my entire mission, discuss the Cuban problem with me. I had only two interviews, each one at my request, with the Secretary. One was before I left for Havana to assume my post as Chief of Mission. The second interview was at the Waldorf-Astoria Hotel in 1959, after I had been recalled from the Havana post. Castro was then in power. Batista had fled Cuba. At that time, the Secretary asked me if I could explain how it happened that Batista lost control to Castro, in view of all the arms and military equipment owned by the Batista government, plus the support of his Air Force. The Secretary again mentioned the friendship to the United States demonstrated by Batista's Ambassador to the United Nations, Dr. Núñez Portuondo. I would not presume to guess the reasons for the Secretary's remarks or his line of thinking. He apparently had not been completely informed as to the background of the Castro brothers until it was too late. This is no criticism of John Foster Dulles. No one man can carry the whole world on his shoulders.

It is a criticism of the structure of the State Department where the attitude of the United States toward a friendly government may be determined through the day-by-day actions of those in the lower echelon. I am convinced, I repeat, that the alternative to Batista need not have been Castro, the Communist. The United States could have been instrumental in forming a broadly-based government in Cuba without Batista and without Castro. In my judgment, it would have been possible to have established such a government up until the summer of 1958. As the months passed after that, it would have been more and more difficult to exclude Castro. Fidel Castro was not the only alternative for Cuba, nor did Castro single-handedly conquer the island of Cuba.

We undermined Batista but failed to encourage a peaceful solution. The Fourth Floor said we hoped for acceptable elections. But we would not support the Church, the political opposition and civic groups to make an all-out effort to create an atmosphere which was conducive to holding honest elections, so that the people of Cuba could select their own government. We would not support a broadly based national unity government, which would have acted only as a provisional government and would have remained in office only long enough to hold general elections.

I have shown in this book that on various occasions, when the timing was propitious and opportunities were available for a solution without Batista or Castro, our Department of State refused to lend its support. The refusal was based on the grounds that the United States would be accused of intervening in the internal affairs of Cuba. Yet, eventually, the State

Department did advise Batista that the time had come for him to absent himself from his country. That was positive intervention on behalf of Castro.

No formula for a successful solution without Castro or Batista could succeed without the support of the United States. The United States held a dominant position in Cuba. The prestige and influence of the United States in Cuba until January 1, 1959, was all important. Only the United States could have implemented a viable solution. No group, except the Church, was bold enough to incur the enmity of both Castro and Batista by trying to put into effect a solution without the active endorsement of the United States. The Church consistently made attempts for a peaceful solution and consistently hoped, without avail, for United States support.

Yet the composite of United States government agencies, the press and members of Congress, through their unsympathetic actions, did so very much to help bring about the overthrow of the Batista dictatorship. Many influential individuals in the State Department were in sympathy with what they believed was a mass revolution taking place in Cuba. These influential individuals were prepared to gamble on a Leftist dictator in order to bring about the downfall of a Rightist dictator. Such a policy cannot be beneficial to the United States.

In our country, there was a general misconception that the events in Cuba were brought about by low standards of living and social inequalities. The facts belie this.

It was not until shortly before Batista fled that I talked to the Under Secretary of State, and not until the fall of 1958 that I was interviewed by the Deputy Under Secretary of State. As far as I know, the decisions were made by the Assistant Secretary of State for Latin American Affairs. My line of communication ran through the Department of State and through the channels of the Department of State. My predecessor, Ambassador Gardner, testified that he was ignored and not even debriefed at the end of his mission. I also was never de-briefed.[1] This is not businesslike procedure; nevertheless, it is what happened.

From my life experience in public service and in business, I have reached the conclusion that the structure of organization in the State Department is faulty by law. No President, no Secretary of State, no matter how sincere and purposeful, can protect the United States from the damage of this day-by-day operation by the lower officials. These men are protected by the Foreign Office Service Law, by the Civil Service Law, by the Veterans Administration Law, and by Congressional pressure. For all practical purposes, they cannot be dismissed. They protect each other as though they belonged to a fraternity.

There is no advantage to the United States in sending an Ambassador to a country if the CIA representatives there act on their own and take an opposite position. The situation becomes especially confused if the CIA representatives send reports back which, following a doctrinaire position, confuse those who sit in Washington. For instance, the Ambassador reports that the present policy of the State Department will only benefit the Communists, the CIA reports that the revolutionary leadership is not Communist-controlled. Who is correct? Do we have to wait for the course of events to establish the truth? That can be very costly.

When the determination of a policy as important as our attitude toward a friendly government arises I believe the President or the National Security Council of the United

[1] It is customary, when the man-on-the-spot returns from his post, to be questioned by the State Department as to his latest views and as to his estimate of the situation. This is what is meant by de-briefing.

States, or some such higher authority, should make the decision. Then the actions of all the departments of the government, including the State Department, should be guided in accordance with such policy as laid down by higher authority. And those who feel that they must go their own way should be asked to leave.

Perhaps the greatest confusion in our foreign relations arises from the uncertainty as to what our policy really is. As an Ambassador, I was never told. The briefings I received from Herbert Matthews and the Fourth Floor certainly did not indicate cordiality to the government of Cuba. It seems to me that when an Ambassador is designated as Chief of Mission to a country he should be given definite briefing as to our policy, its permanent features and its flexibility—certainly about the country to which he is sent. The fact that an Ambassador these days is at the end of a telephone does not matter. In a revolution communications may be cut off.

Non-intervention in the internal affairs of other nations has allegedly been the cornerstone of our foreign policy; yet for the United States to proclaim non-intervention in the affairs of Cuba was not realistic. Cuba was too close to the United States historically, economically, socially, and geographically not to be affected by the daily occurrences in the United States. The United States intervened every day, in one form or another, in Cuban affairs. The Cuban government recognized this; the Cuban people were aware of this.

The State Department does not admit its error regarding the Castro Communist revolution. In April 1961, sixteen months after Castro assumed control of the government of Cuba, the Department of State released its White Paper on Cuba, which speaks of "The Betrayal of the Cuban Revolution" and states: "Never in history has any revolution so rapidly devoured its children." The opening statement of the White Paper is as follows:

(232)

What Does It All Mean?

The present situation in Cuba confronts the Western Hemisphere and the Inter-American system with a grave and urgent challenge.

This challenge does not result from the fact that the Castro government in Cuba was established by revolution. The hemisphere rejoiced at the overthrow of the Batista tyranny, looked with sympathy on the new regime, and welcomed its promises of political freedom and social justice for the Cuban people. The challenge results from the fact that the leaders of the revolutionary regime betrayed their own revolution, delivered that revolution into the hands of powers alien to the hemisphere, and transformed it into an instrument employed with calculated effect to suppress the rekindled hopes of the Cuban people for democracy and to intervene in the internal affairs of other American Republics.

What began as a movement to enlarge Cuban democracy and freedom has been perverted, in short, into a mechanism for the destruction of free institutions in Cuba, for the seizure by international communism of a base and bridgehead in the Americas, and for the disruption of the Inter-American system.

Further, the White Paper says: "When Doctor Castro decided to betray the promises of the Revolution, he had to liquidate the instrumentalities which embodied those promises and to destroy the men who took the promises seriously."

Many people may have been sincerely misled by Castro, but the Department of State cannot afford to be misled. The Fourth Floor was fully informed on Fidel Castro since the 1948 Bogotá uprising.

The Fourth Floor should not have been so naïve as to believe that the Communists would not take advantage of the 26th of July Movement as they saw fit. The Fourth Floor should not have been so naïve as to brush off all reports on Communist infiltration and Communist control of the Castro movement as being Batista propaganda.

The State Department and the Central Intelligence Agency

(233)

were aware that Che Guevara was an active Communist in Guatemala and Mexico and that Raúl Castro had been active in the international Communist student movement.

The White Paper, I believe, further substantiates my contention that these influential individuals on the Fourth Floor were even prepared to gamble on a Leftist dictator in order to have the revolution succeed. Furthermore, they had the reports in their files of Fidel Castro's Communist affiliations provided by United States Ambassadors to Cuba, Mexico, probably Colombia, and many other sources.

On May 1, 1961, less than one month after the release of the White Paper, the Cuban Premier, Fidel Castro, in a three and a half hour television address at a May Day gathering in Havana, declared that Cuba was a Socialist country and would no longer hold elections. In the future, Castro said, his regime would depend on direct support by Cubans attending similar rallys.

"Do you need elections?" Castro asked the crowd. "No, no" his audience shouted. Castro said the revolution does not contemplate giving the oppressive class any chance to return to power. Then he said: "If Mr. Kennedy does not like Socialism, we don't like imperialism. We don't like capitalism." He warned the United States' aggressive policies were putting New York in danger of becoming another Hiroshima.

Lincoln White, press officer of the State Department, declared the Castro May Day speech proclaiming Cuba a Socialist state shows that Cuba has certainly become a member of the Communist bloc.

In a nationwide radio-television address on December 2, 1961, Fidel Castro said: "I am a Marxist-Leninist and will be one until the day I die." The rest of the world is "on the way to Communism." He also said that he was forming a single Communist-like "United Party of Cuba's Socialist Revolution." The new party would lead Cuba through Socialism to "a people's democracy or the dictatorship of the proletariat." Its program will be "Marxist-Leninist and adapted to conditions in Cuba." Then he goes on to say, "There is no halfway between Socialism and imperialism."

Surely it is difficult to understand why the higher echelon of the State Department, as late as April 1961, permitted release of the White Paper on Cuba.

The United States cannot afford to excuse such costly mistakes by saying that the revolution was betrayed by Castro. The United States cannot afford to risk its security by having the Fourth Floor gamble on a Leftist dictator in order to have revolutions succeed.

The motivation of the Fourth Floor must be regarded as unselfish. However, we cannot assume that in a changing world the United States can support revolutionary groups which call themselves Democratic but are in reality Marxist oriented. If it is our fixed policy to support Democratic revolutions, then it is our obligation to intervene to assure that they are Democratic and not Communist, otherwise we defeat our own idealistic purposes. It is the function of the State Department and the CIA to know in advance the nature of each revolutionary group. The United States risks its survival on such knowledge.

It is a fact that we have a Communist country ninety miles off our shores. There is a possibility that the Caribbean might become a Communist lake. It is our duty and obligation to prevent such a possibility.

Index

Index

Index

ABOUT THE AUTHOR

Financier, corporate director, and Member of the New York Stock Exchange for more than thirty years, EARL E. T. SMITH attended Taft School and Yale University. A man who has loved the sea since his birth in Newport, Rhode Island, Mr. Smith now lives by the ocean in Florida, where he has been active in both state and national politics.

During World War II the author served overseas as a lieutenant colonel in the United States Army and United States 8th Air Force Intelligence. His government career has been distinguished by appointments from three Presidents: as Chief of Field Offices, Contract Distribution Division, War Production Board before Pearl Harbor, by Franklin D. Roosevelt; as Ambassador to Cuba from 1957 to 1959, by Dwight D. Eisenhower; and as Ambassador to Switzerland (later declined), by John F. Kennedy.